THE INFLUENCE OF
SPECIALIZED TRAINING ON TESTS
OF GENERAL INTELLIGENCE

BY

KATHARINE B. GRAVES, PH.D.

TEACHERS COLLEGE, COLUMBIA UNIVERSITY
CONTRIBUTIONS TO EDUCATION, NO. 143

Published by
Teachers College, Columbia University
New York City
1924

Library of Congress Cataloging in Publication Data

Graves, Katharine Bradford, 1897–
    The influence of specialized training on tests of
general intelligence.

    Reprint of the 1924 ed., issued in series: Teachers
College, Columbia University. Contributions to education, no. 143.
    Originally presented as the author's thesis, Columbia.

    1. Mental tests. I. Title. II. Series: Columbia
University. Teachers College. Contributions to
education, no. 143.
BF431.G763 1972   153.9'32   73-176818
ISBN 0-404-55143-2

Reprinted by Special Arrangement with Teachers
College Press, New York, New York

From the edition of 1924, New York
First AMS edition published in 1972
Manufactured in the United States

AMS PRESS, INC.
NEW YORK, N. Y.   10003

PREFACE

THE work reported in this monograph was inspired by the interest and encouragement of Dr. Edward L. Thorndike and Dr. Leta S. Hollingworth. Doctor Hollingworth further guided the course of the experiment from its start as a vague problem to its completion as a piece of definite research.

My thanks are also due the principals of the schools where this work was done, and the mental examiners whose kindly attitude was encouraging at a time when the amount of testing to be completed in a short period called for the co-operation of all.

KATHARINE B. GRAVES

CONTENTS

THE INFLUENCE OF SPECIALIZED TRAINING ON TESTS OF GENERAL INTELLIGENCE

CHAPTER I

INTRODUCTION

If we follow the lines of intelligence tests, as differentiated from educational tests, we find them divided into group and individual forms of examination. Most of the more useful group examinations have duplicate forms which help to avoid, so far as is possible, the practice effects from repetition of exactly the same tests. But individual examination forms are harder to standardize since results can be gained only one at a time. An alternative form means much more labor. Thus there is no individual examination with an alternative form whose results are equivalent to the first form.

This condition exposes individual examinations to a peril less often felt in the field of group testing. It is no uncommon experience in New York City for a mental examiner in an out-patient clinic to be faced with a child who has been tested at least twice in the preceding month. In all places where mental tests are a regular part of the program, the influence of coaching is frequently suspected by the investigator.

In the experience of most investigators[1] a child does seem to gain in mental age by a repetition of the test within a short period. Such influence is probably fourfold in cause. The gain may be due to actual solving of the problem, which the child recalls after leaving the examination; it may be due to less timidity on the part of the child or perhaps due to the adaptation of better mental set in which the child meets the situation the second time. In the second case, there is more or less casual conversation between the children which may help the child. This influence is

[1] Rugg and Colloton, "Constancy of the Stanford-Binet I. Q. as Shown by Re-tests." *Journal of Educational Psychology,* September 1921.

probably slight, but it is present. One child being faced with the ball and field test of year VIII,[2] remarked, without waiting for complete directions, "I know; you go 'round and 'round to the middle," and therewith gave a "superior plan" for the solution of that problem, when it was probable that he would not have achieved this score without assistance. In another case, a crude but effective series of drawings was found in the laundry room of an institution for the care of feeble-minded, depicting human heads each with a defect carefully labeled. These defects or omissions were intended to help those who could not see the defects for themselves, as the labels were read out to the low-grade inmates.

In the third case, not all teachers prove as circumspect in their relations to the tests as we who deal in them may wish. To many teachers, the tests merely represent another hurdle over which they must conduct their children, if they are to do their full duty by their charges. Even when the teacher is convinced that the particular test must be kept sacred to the psychological laboratory, she is likely to feel that the material may be used well in her classroom if it is altered ever so slightly.

And in the last place, parents and guardians of children have sometimes felt the need of aiding the child, of preparing him for the trial which he is to face, of keeping him from an unjust discrimination against him. All this can be done, in their opinion, by "stuffing" the child with the answers to the stunts which have been so arbitrarily imposed upon him. Even those who realize the true significance of the test may feel that in the case of their own child, such conditions may be altered. There is one mother who learned to give and evaluate the results of the more usual forms of mental tests. But she said of her own son that no one should ever grade him by any rule of thumb if she could help it. She had coached him at the age of three so that she was sure he could pass most of the tests up to year twelve.

Such cases as these are sporadic. But they do point out a field which needs investigation. Can we say that results are comparable, when two children represent two different school environ-

---

[2] Stanford Revision of the Binet-Simon Tests. Copyright, 1916, by Houghton Mifflin Company.

ments? Terman feels that there is little difference due to the factor of dissimilar school experience, within certain limits.[3]

How much effect on the child's score can we expect from school work similar to the tests? How far can a child be coached by persons of more mature intelligence? And, in either case, how long will these effects endure?

It was to answer these three questions in some degree that this particular research was undertaken.

---

[3] Terman, L. M., *The Measurement of Intelligence.* Houghton Mifflin Company, 1916.

CHAPTER II

PRELIMINARY EXPERIMENT

Investigation was begun in the early fall of 1921. Arrangements were made with a nearby institution which is always ready to be of service in any scientific work.

Children were tested with the Stanford Revision of the Binet-Simon tests at the time of entrance into the quarantine or reception hall. Here they were kept for six weeks, during which time the examiner could call for them singly or in small groups. After considerable testing twelve children were found whose mental and chronological ages corresponded fairly well.

These twelve were divided into three groups and experimentation was begun. One group, hereafter referred to as the "control" group, was left alone, and no attempts were made to influence their training between the two times of testing.

The second group was practised on material that was similar in nature to the work of the tests in the Stanford Revision of the Binet-Simon Tests. This group will hereafter be referred to, in this investigation, as the "similar" group. The four children in this group were given booklets made out by the examiner which contained material thought to be similar to the twenty-four tests of the years VI through IX inclusive. These children were helped and the particular difficulties of the tests explained by the examiner so that at the end of the third group training period three of the children seemed to have control of the material. On the following day the fourth child was called to the office and given individual help with the problems he found difficult. This whole period of training lasted a week.

During this same week the members of the third group were given their coaching, at another period. The tests themselves were the material for the group training. Thus, this group had the more direct coaching, and will from now on be called the "coached" group. The correct answers were told the children, for each test, and practice and drill were given to teach them to

4

the children as thoroughly as the time allowed. They enjoyed the work and showed signs of rivalry. Three of this group were considered to have gained the maximum under the conditions at the end of the third period. The fourth child was given additional help on the next day.

The re-tests were given as closely together as was possible. Just at this time the children were moved to another building, so there was some difficulty in getting them promptly.

At the end of three months from the first test, two months after the re-test following the training period, the tests were repeated. At the end of a year from the original test, the tests were given for the fourth time.

The control group, having an average mental age of 84 months in the first test, averaged two months of gain in mental age in the first interval; gained nothing in three months beyond its original standing; and lost on the average one month in the year between its first and fourth tests. During these same periods, the group known as "similar" shows different results, due to the training given between the first and second test. The "similar" group had an average mental age of 87 months in the first test; gained twelve months as an average in the test following training; retained on an average seven months' improvement during the three-month interval; and still had an average of four months' advance over its original standing at the end of a year. The "coached" group also made some improvement on the later test. The first average mental age found for the "coached" group was 84 months, and the average gain in the second test was nine months; the group retained five months of this improvement on the average, in the third test, and still had an average gain of one month, at the end of the year, over the original standing.

The results are also given in the following table. The errors are probably large, the group is indubitably too small to offer any reliable results, but still this work was valuable. It opened the way for further work and showed many places where improved methods of coaching might bring better results.

The gains in all these cases are calculated after subtracting from the second score (the crude result as obtained by the re-test) the number of months which have elapsed between tests. In this way allowance is made for the gain in score due merely to the lapse of time. This is the only method which does not call into play the disputable idea of I.Q. and the differing allowances to be made for differing I.Q.'s in the same period.

TABLE I

THE RESULTS OF TRAINING IN A PRELIMINARY COACHING EXPERIMENT: STATED IN TERMS OF MENTAL AGE*

Control Group				Similar Group				Coached Group			
M.A. I Test	Gain II-I	Gain III-I	Gain IV-I	M.A. I Test	Gain II-I	Gain III-I	Gain IV-L	M.A. I Test	Gain II-I	Gain III-I	Gain IV-I
a 92	4	−3	−10	e 94	17	16	13	i 92	9	13	9
b 86	1	3	0	f 92	5	2	−1	j 86	11	−1	X
c 87	0	4	−1	g 84	13	1	−1	k 84	7	5	1
d 70	2	−3	8	h 77	12	8	X	l 76	9	3	−6
335(4	7	1	−3	347(4	47	27	11(3	338(4	36	20	4(3
84	2	0	−1	87	12	7	4	84	9	5	1

* This table reads as follows: Child *a* in the control group, tested at 92 months mental age at the first test. He had gained 4 months mental age by the next test, (he had lost 3 months by the third test,) and had lost 10 months at the fourth test. These were the results after subtracting the amount of growth which would normally have occurred in the period intervening between tests.

CHAPTER III

ORGANIZATION

The next step was the organizing of the material for presentation to a larger group, and the location of such a group.

In the Appendix will be found a copy of form "I" of the material used in training the group referred to as the "similar"[1] group. The sources of the material, the instructions accompanying the giving of the tests, and the answers which were accepted from the children are all given at that point. The other two forms used in training these children are variations of this one.

This training is intended to parallel the tests, from years VI to X inclusive, of the Stanford Revision of the Binet-Simon Tests. This is one year more (six tests more) than was used in the training of the first group, for the results from this preliminary experiment were indicative of ability on the part of children of these mental ages to learn more than had been taught. There are now thirty tests in the Stanford Revision which are paralleled by this method of training. One of these tests—the vocabulary test of year VIII, test 6—is repeated with higher requirements in year X, test 1, so that by leaving out this repetition, the training consisted of twenty-nine parts.

The group referred to as the "coached" group—that is, those who were trained on the tests and their answers directly—was also trained under a more detailed plan. This plan is given in the Appendix. Limits were set for the time to be given to each part, the answers were strictly defined, and the type of practice to be used was established.

There were two considerations which decided these limits and methods. There was only a limited amount of time which could be used for this work; and the preliminary work had shown that tests differed in requiring different amounts of time for learning

---

[1] The "similar" group means those children who were given training in the material thought to be similar to the tests, but not identical with them. The tests referred to are those tests from years VI to X inclusive of the Stanford Revision of the Binet-Simon Tests.

7

by those children capable of grasping them. Failure to draw the correct response for the ball and field test (year VIII, test 1)[2] at the end of five minutes means that the child would probably be still unable to draw it at the expenditure of a greater length of time; while for him to be unable to copy the diamond (VII-6) at the end of five minutes may mean that he will not grasp the principle at the end of fifteen minutes, but the chances are one out of three that ten minutes' longer practice will give him control of the process.

The selection of groups where this work could be carried on was very difficult. In the first place, it was thought to be simpler to have all three groups in the school. Not only would it be a great deal easier administratively, but it was almost impossible to find three schools where the home environment of the children could be considered equivalent. It was considered wiser to get these children from a neighborhood where there would be little chance that the parents of the children would coach them. That meant that what is referred to in real estate terms as "the better residential district" could not be considered a good field for investigation. The combination of more education and more leisure for the mothers produces a closer interest in the school welfare of the child. This interest is helpful in regular teaching and school administration, but it often leads to too partial a view of the child's experiences to preserve the impartiality of an experiment.

Nor could we select a group where there were many children who had come to this country within the last two or so years. While Miss Bere's work[3] shows that length of stay in the country is not correlated with the standing achieved from intelligence tests, still it was thought advisable to cut off from consideration all those who had been here less than four years.

The experiment was to be carried on in as elementary a school grade as possible, in order to minimize the effect of school environment, and so that there would be little chance that any child should be able to do the majority of the tests which were to be taught in these groups. The first grade is a poor grade

---

[2] All such references, year given in Roman numerals, test in Arabic, are to refer to the Stanford Revision of the Binet-Simon Test, denoting the various tests, as is done there.

[3] An unpublished thesis by Miss May Bere at Teachers College, Columbia University.

TABLE II

CORRELATION BETWEEN AVERAGE LENGTH OF RESIDENCE OF PARENTS, AND
MENTAL CAPACITY OF CHILDREN
[*From study by May Bere*]

Race	Correlation between Residence and Stanford Binet M. A.	Correlation between Residence and Pintner-Patterson M. A.
Italian	−.063	−.016
Bohemian	−.034	−.037
Hebrew	−.03	.16

100 ten-year-old boys were used for each group.

to do this work in, for children are started there, however great
their inaptitude, and are generally kept there for a year, however
great their abilities. Further, the range of mental age is too large
to make comparisons easy. So the second grade was selected for
this test.

There are several requirements which a school must meet, in
order to be a satisfactory one for the experiment. The school shall
be one where the principal and teachers are willing to co-operate
with the tester; it must have at least three second grades, which
are not differentiated one from the other in any strict fashion;
the children shall all come from similar home environments, from
families that have been in this country at least four years, and
interest on the part of the parents must not be great enough, or
partial enough, to interfere with the conditions of the experiment.

These requirements were met at two schools which will hereafter be referred to as A and Y. There was supposedly no
differentiation, except by chance, at school A. At school Y one
group was held to be better than the other two since no children
who had failed of promotion from the second grade the preceding
June were in it. This differentiation did have an effect on the
average mental age[4] of the group, but it did not affect the amount
gained by the different groups as distinguished from the gains
they would have made had they had an equal mental age, if we
can draw any conclusions from the smallness of the correlations
in all groups between the original mental age and the gains made

---

[4] Throughout the "original mental age" or "mental age" is held to refer
to the results of the first test, as reckoned by directions on pages 39 ff. of
The Measurement of Intelligence by L. M. Terman.

in the second test results over the first test results. The average mental age, and the correlations between this original score and subsequent learning, are presented in Tables III and IIIA respectively.

TABLE III

AVERAGE MENTAL AGE AND I. Q. OF THE GROUPS IN THE EXPERIMENT, GIVEN TO THE NEAREST HALF-POINT

	Control Group		Coached Group		Similar Group		Average	
	Average	S.D. of Dist.	Average	S.D. of Dist.	Average	S.D. of Dist.	Average	S.D. of Dist.
School A								
Mental Age..........	87.20(25)	9.43	86.66(29)	8.09	92.04(24)	7.85	88.48(78)	8.53
Chronological Age.....	97.80(25)	14.26	100.79(29)	11.14	96.38 (24)	16.90	98.47(78)	14.35
I.Q................	90.56(25)	13.60	86.72(29)	10.40	97.79(24)	14.29	91.36(78)	13.58
School Y								
Mental Age..........	84.57(28)	7.81	88.43(21)	6.06	94.92(26)	10.39	89.24(75)	8.76
Chronological Age.....	88.61(28)	4.96	92.38(21)	5.11	89.69(26)	5.56	90.04(75)	5.57
I.Q................	95.85(28)	10.60	96.24(21)	10.01	106.46(26)	12.26	99.64(75)	12.28
Combined A and Y								
Mental Age..........	85.81(53)	5.44	87.40(50)	7.43	93.54(50)	10.31	88.85(153)	8.64
Chronological Age.....	92.94(53)	11.31	97.26(50)	9.97	92.90(50)	12.69	94.34(153)	11.73
I.Q................	93.36(53)	12.41	90.72(50)	10.26	102.30(50)	13.88	95.41(153)	13.64

Throughout this study the numbers in parentheses ( ) in the tables give the number of cases which are represented in the averages, sigmas, etc., immediately preceding.

TABLE IIIA

CORRELATION BETWEEN THE ORIGINAL MENTAL AGE AND THE AMOUNT GAINED; COMPUTED BY SUBTRACTING FIRST MENTAL AGE FROM MENTAL AGE GIVEN BY SECOND TEST

School	Control Group		Coached Group		Similar Group	
	r	σ	r	σ	r	σ
A..........	−.26	9.43	.18	8.09	−.12	7.85
Y..........	0	7.81	.20	6.06	−.38	10.39

The σ is the σ of distribution of the original m.a. given in months.
The results of the second score are made comparable to those of the first score by eliminating the influence of time and tester by the process described on p. 17.

The correlations between the original mental age and the amount gained by coaching are so small as to show little effect from the original mental age on the amount learned, at least within these bounds.

This correlation may be reduced because of the limited number of tests which are coached. A child with a high mental age did not have a chance to learn so many tests as did a child with a lower mental age. At school A, for example, a child with a mental age of eight had a chance to learn twelve tests, while a child with a mental age of seven had eighteen tests in which he could make some improvement. If the number of coached tests had been larger, the correlation between mental age and "improvement due to coaching" might have been larger in a positive direction. This is not a powerful agent so far as we can find any evidence. The children at Y were coached in eight more tests than the children at A, yet the correlation is only .20 as compared with a correlation of .18 at A. That is, the chance to gain twenty-four more months of mental age resulted in no greater improvement, practically, for the children at the upper levels than for those at the lower levels.

The sigmas of the distribution vary from six to ten months of mental age, while the actual variations of average mental age vary less than six months from the average of the group. When these groups are combined, as they may well be because of their essential similarity at the start, the groups are even more alike in original ability. Here we have a difference of four and a half months as the greatest difference between the average of any sub-group and the group as a whole.

These tests were given over a period of two school years. The first testing and training program was put through in one school in January and February, and in the second school during May, with a few days in June. There was only one holiday occurring in this period. This one came during the latter part of the work when the co-operation of the children was well established. All of those who were expected came with one exception. The results from this child were dropped, since there was no way of testing her at the time set. Since the children did not have to take examinations, there was no upheaval of the regular school routine by the approach of the final weeks. In this respect the conditions were as normal as could be expected.

The nationality of the children was disregarded. There were twelve different nationalities represented at school Y alone, and they were fairly divided by chance among the three groups. The two nationalities most frequently claimed were Austrian and Russian, and these numbered about twenty children for each nationality at this school. Thus the groups are too small to isolate satisfactorily, while they are so well distributed that any effect they might have had is lost by chance arrangement. The home language is an interesting study. All of these children talk English to the other children at play, and say that they talk English to their brothers and sisters. But the language they use with their parents may differ from home to home. There is one case in each class at Y where the only language used at home is English. In all other cases they speak a foreign language as well, and in a few cases, two foreign languages. Table IV gives a comparison of the groups, but there are so few cases that no conclusions can be drawn from the data.

TABLE IV

AVERAGE MENTAL AGE AND I. Q. FOR GROUPS OF DIFFERENT NATIONALITIES

Nationality	Average M. A.	S. D. of Distribution	Average I. Q.	S. D. of Distribution
Italian (19)	85.16	11.45	86.74	12.07
Russian (58)	96.29	7.14	95.51	10.68
Austrian (30)	84.23	8.09	98.60	10.42

AVERAGE MENTAL AGE AND I. Q. FOR GROUPS SPEAKING LANGUAGES OTHER THAN ENGLISH IN THE HOME

Italian (15)	86.67	11.88	87.20	11.65
Russian (32)	81.31	6.86	93.81	8.63
Yiddish (39)	87.26	6.55	99.26	9.61

AVERAGE MENTAL AGE AND I. Q. FOR GROUP SPEAKING ENGLISH AT HOME

English (41)	90.46	7.69	93.97	7.46

The other nationalities and language groups are not large enough to be reliable at all.

The results for the sexes are given separately in Table V. There is in no group a difference of four months' mental age, and as the "control" group presents a gain of almost this size at a re-test given three weeks after the first test, we need no other cause than chance for the sex differences found.

TABLE V

AVERAGE MENTAL AGE AND GAINS FOR THE THREE GROUPS, DISTRIBUTED
BY SEX
Given in Months of Mental Age

	Original Average Mental Age	S. D. of Distribution	Average Gain II-I
Control Group:			
Boys..................	86.26 (27)	10.04	2.19
Girls..................	85.35 (26)	7.04	4.00
Coached A:			
Boys..................	86.38 (13)	9.92	23.92
Girls..................	87.25 (16)	7.04	22.44
Coached Y:			
Boys..................	84 (7)	2.56	35.00
Girls..................	90.64 (14)	6.15	30.07
Coached A and Y			
Boys..................	85.55 (20)	8.02	....
Girls..................	88.63 (30)	6.62	....
Similar:			
Boys..................	91.45 (22)	6.23	5.91
Girls..................	95.18 (28)	7.84	6.57
Average M. A.:			
Boys..................	87.71 (69)	8.79	....
Girls..................	89.87 (84)	8.25	....
Combined...........	88.89 (153)	8.57	

As to whether there is any other cause than chance at work, the authorities are divided. Terman feels that there is a small but constant difference, in favor of the girls. He gives a table of the results of Miss Cuneo's work with kindergarten children that shows a difference in the group tested.[5] There were in the group 65 boys, and 47 girls. The median chronological age for the boys was about five years, three months (calculated from his summary table), and for girls the median chronological age was about five years and five months. The table itself is given in terms of I.Q. points.

On the other hand Yerkes[6] feels that a great deal of emphasis should be placed on sex differences in test achievements, although

[5] Terman, L. M., *Intelligence of School Children.*
[6] Yerkes, Bridges, and Hardwick, *A Point Scale for Measuring Mental Ability.* Warwick and York, 1915.

TABLE VI

RESULTS OF MISS CUNEO'S WORK REPORTED IN I. Q. POINTS
112 KINDERGARTEN CHILDREN
65 Boys   47 Girls
After Terman

	Median	Lower Quartile	Upper Quartile
Boys..............	103	90	114
Girls..............	108	96.5	116.5

his norms for the two sexes lie close together at any age, and repeatedly cross each other. He feels that reliance may be placed on these results, though the groups are obviously small. The sex norms for the combined language groups as found by Yerkes are given in Table VII. It would seem that his table supports Terman's arguments fairly well.

TABLE VII

TABLE II OF YERKES (*op. cit.*)
AVERAGE SCORES FOR THE SEX AND AGE GROUPS OF SCHOOL B

Age.........	4(5)	5(30)	6(71)	7(73)	8(61)	9(74)
Boys........	15	20	28	32	41	52
Girls........	9	24	30	33	36	54

Age.........10(76)	11(79)	12(60)	13(60)	14(52)	15(25)
Boys........ 62	64	71	73	80	78
Girls........ 58	63	75	76	77	76

Kuhlmann[7] makes no mention of sex differences in any way, grouping the results together without reference to sex. Terman,[8] in the book on the Stanford Revision, has made some interesting suggestions. On page 68 he says, "The question as to the relative intelligence of the sexes is one of perennial interest and great social importance. The ancient hypothesis, the one which dates from the time when men only concerned themselves with scientific hypotheses, took for granted the superiority of the male. With the development of individual psychology, however, it was soon found that so far as the evidence of mental tests can be trusted

[7] F. Kuhlmann, *A Handbook of Mental Tests.* Warwick and York, 1922.
[8] *The Measurement of Intelligence.*

the *average* intelligence of women and girls is as high as that of men and boys. Let us see what our 1000 I.Q.'s have to offer toward a solution of the problem.

"1. When the I.Q.'s of the boys and girls were treated separately there was found a small but fairly constant superiority of the girls up to the age of thirteen years. At fourteen, however, the curve for the girls dropped below that for boys. (This may be due to the more frequent elimination of the brighter 14-year-old girls from the grades by promotion to the High School.)

"2. However, the superiority of girls over boys is so slight (amounting at most ages to only two or three points in terms of I.Q.) that for practical purposes it would seem negligible. This offers no support to the opinion expressed by Yerkes and Bridges that 'at certain ages serious injustice will be done individuals by evaluating their score in the light of norms which do not take account of sex differences.'

"3. Apart from the small superiority of girls, the distribution of intelligence in the two sexes is not different. The supposed wider variation of boys is not found. Girls do not group themselves about the median more closely than do boys. The range of I.Q. including the middle fifty per cent is approximately the same for the two sexes.

"4. When the results for the individual tests were examined, it was found that not many showed very extreme differences, as to the per cent of boys and girls passing."

Burt[9] says on page 193, "The two sexes, indeed, seem during their intellectual progress to be playing a sort of statistical leap-frog, now one dip, now the other, throughout their whole school course. Even here (i.e., the linguistic tests where girls are more superior than in other tests), rarely, if ever, do the differences of boys and girls reach the equivalent of half a year. Hence to compile age-norms for the two sexes separately seems hardly needful."

The last conclusion of Terman, as to the small difference in the percentage of boys passing a test compared to the percentage of girls passing the same test, was found to hold in this experiment. Such detailed results will be taken up at another time.

The environment of these children ranks at about average. They come, almost uniformly, from homes where the father is a me-

---

[9] Cyril Burt, *Mental and Scholastic Tests.* P. S. King and Sons, Ltd., 1922.

chanic, skilled laborer, or a small shop manager. In the case of each school, the neighborhood from which it draws its children is uniform. There is no mixture of poorer and better grade homes in the district. There was no mixture of two or more social groups in the school enrollment. The children have been born in this country, or have come here under three years of age; they are all children of foreign-born parents, and come from homes where Americanization is taking place, though slowly in some cases.

CHAPTER IV

ADMINISTRATION

Those who served as examiners for this work were all unusually well prepared. All five of those used were college graduates who had taken graduate courses in psychology. All of them were trained in the giving of the Stanford Revision of the Binet-Simon Tests. All scores and results were re-checked by the experimenter three times, so that there is no variation in the results of one examiner as compared with another, due to errors of calculation. The results are reliable in that respect.

The influence of the tester on the scores obtained from the children she tested or re-tested was subtracted from their score. Thus the average gain for a group was determined, and the average gain for the children scored by each tester was also found. The average difference between these two scores was calculated, and subtracted from each of the individual scores recorded by that tester. In this way whatever influence the tester may have had on the results was effectively cleared away, and the results were such as would have been obtained by the course of training if only one examiner had given all of the tests and re-tests. No examiner re-tested (in the second test) any child whom she had had in the first test. In this way any bias was kept out of the results, and by dividing the children which any tester had had, between the other two testers at the time of the re-test, it was possible to make an accurate estimate of the children's gains and losses apart from any tendency on the part of one examiner to score higher or lower than the other two. In this way all the results were reduced to a common basis, unaffected by the temperament of the tester.

The children were tested thoroughly over a larger range than is usual. Instructions were given to start all tests at six years, going lower if necessary, and to carry all tests through two years beyond the last year where a score of more than one test was

17

secured. If this meant that the child would not be examined in year ten at school A, or year twelve at school Y, the tester was told to continue the work unless there was every indication that there would be no gain from this further testing. At A for the twenty-five cases in the "control" group there were only four months of gains in the unexplored regions above the years tested, and at Y for the "control" group of twenty-eight cases, there were no gains. For these same groups there were eight months lost in the years below the tests that were given, six months lost at A and two at Y. There was one more safeguard against insufficient exploration. Whenever a repeated test (as a vocabulary or digit memory span) was passed, the child was tried out on the next higher level for that performance, even though every test in the preceding year was completely failed.

The slight amount of gain and loss in the unexplored regions seems conclusive evidence that the testing was thorough in both groups. By going one year farther than Terman recommends we caught almost every case, and the exceptions are more likely to have been real gains than errors because the tester stopped too soon. This method proved satisfactory for comparisons with re-tests taken three and four months later, showing the growth in those months apart from such errors of administration. It is probably better to be as thorough as this in any case where future comparisons are to be made, though Terman lays down lower limits for the minimum essential.

ADMINISTRATION

The administration of the experiment as a whole will next be considered. This will be presented in the order of time in which it was actually given.

At A the preliminary testing was started on Monday and concluded Friday afternoon. Since not every child in the second grade could be tested, the children were selected alphabetically. The list for each tester was so made out that she tested one-third of each class-group tested by the team of three testers. The name of the child, the time of day when tested, and the name of the tester were recorded for future reference in assigning these children to testers for the second test.

At night the work was checked up, and all doubtful responses discussed, so that there was a general agreement as to results. Each tester knew that if there were any question as to the values of responses, she was to record full observations, and continue with further exploration to the year above or below, if such procedure was indicated.

The next two weeks were devoted to the training of the children in the groups known as "similar"[1] and "coached."[1]

The material[2] was made up in the form of small booklets of separate sheets, clipped together with a paper clip. The material was in three forms, known as "a," "b," and "c."

The presenting of this material to the "similar" group was spread over two school weeks. On Monday morning of the first week, the "a" form booklets were presented and the children told to do as well as they could on all of the games, without referring to each other or to the teacher. In the afternoon, another set of "a" form booklets was distributed. In this case the material was presented as before, except that the children replied orally, when called upon ; a good answer was selected, and this correct answer dictated by the tester to the children, who filled in the test blanks. If any of the answers were difficult or hard for the children to spell, the class-room teacher wrote or drew it on the board where all the children could see and copy it. During this period there was considerable discussion by the children. They felt free to make suggestions, and took an interest in getting the correct answers.

On Wednesday and Friday of this same week forms "b" and "c" were presented in similar fashion, morning and afternoon. These booklets were variants of the same material presented in "a." The next week the forms "a," "b" and "c" were given out on Monday, Wednesday, and Friday morning, respectively. The children did the work without asking for help from the teacher or tester.

As it took about an hour and three-quarters to give one of these group forms, the children were given a recess of fifteen minutes

---

[1] "Similar" refers to the group who were given training as a group on material similar to, but not identical with, the tests in years VI to X inclusive in the Stanford Revision of the Binet-Simon Tests ; while "coached" refers to that group who were practised on the correct responses to the tests actually involved, the range being from years VI to X inclusive as in the other group.

[2] The sources used for this are given on pages 51 ff. and the material itself is presented there.

at the end of the first hour. Interest in the test did not wane throughout the period. The children were still ready to go on at the end, though by that time most of the tests were too hard for the majority of them unaided.

The time not spent in giving this training to the "similar" group in this two weeks' period was spent in coaching the group referred to as "coached." The children were all glad to come early, and have the added social prestige of going into the school before the regular opening time. They were seemingly as willing to stay as late as desired. The experimenter was not confined to the regular school hours, but was able to start work at about eight-fifteen, and carry the training through until four or four-thirty in the afternoon. Because of the children's interest in the "games," more was accomplished than would have been possible in a school whose children had more home interests and diversion. In only one case was there any question from a parent as to the child's actions. She was very glad to have the child continue as soon as the matter was explained.

As may be noted, there is a time limit set to the amount of training for each test.[3] This was in each case such time as seemed best to the experimenter to devote to the purpose. There are some cases where it might have been advisable to lengthen the time, but the experimenter felt that if the child did not learn the test in the assigned time, it was improbable that he would learn it without the expenditure of more time than was available for this purpose. All such decisions were based on direct observation. While they are open to modification, the experimenter feels that they are reliable as a basis for the work here undertaken.

The coaching period was divided into periods of group and individual coaching. Three or four children of similar mental age were taken in a group and coached on each test in which they had failed, until two or three were able to give the correct answer, and it seemed a waste of time to keep the successful children waiting while the other child was practised. Each child was then scored plus or minus on his ability to pass this particular test at that time, and the group was directed to the next 'failed' test.

The second period each child had to himself for practice on his own failures. If he seemed to grasp the right answer before

---

[3] See Appendix for this material, and its treatment.

the time allotted that problem was gone, he was graded plus, and no further reference was made to that test during the period. In the third period the child was taken back over his original failures, and practised once more on those he still missed. In this way the time allotted to each test was spread out to avoid fatigue and also to re-impress those answers which were almost but not quite learned.

The groups were taken in the ascending order of their mental age; the group with the highest mental ages was the last practised. For the individual coaching, however, the children were called in the order of their original tests, so that each child tested on Monday was given his last coaching on the Monday two weeks later, while his first re-test fell just three weeks after the first test, and one week after his final individual coaching. This rule was impossible to follow in two cases, where one child was tested a day late, and a corresponding child a day early, due to the absence of the first child.

The material used in A and Y for coaching purposes was the same, except that the children at Y had an extra year of material, and were coached on years VI and XII inclusive, while those at A were coached on years VI to X inclusive. The work at A showed that some of the children in the second grade could be successfully coached higher than had been attempted, so that this extra series of tests was added for the work at Y. Otherwise the administration of the coaching was the same. The results are presented for the total scores, the scores for years VI to X and years VI to XII inclusive, so that the reader may make his own conclusions based on the material as presented in these three comparative tables.

On the Monday following the two weeks of intermediate work, the three testers started re-testing the children examined during the first week. Each examiner re-tested one-half of the children first tested by each of the other examiners. No child was re-tested by the same examiner. Moreover, each examiner tested one-third of the children in each group, so that any tendency on her part to mark too high or too low was allowed for in the actual results of the children (further allowance was made for this as previously explained on page 17). The children were re-tested on the same day of the week as before, thus making a period of exactly three weeks between tests, with the one exception already noted.

All of the evidence which has been examined shows that the

time of school day taken for the test has no effect, or so small an effect as to be negligible.   In order to make constant the effects which we might get from testing outside of school hours as well as during that period, and to equalize any loss of interest in the work from this cause, the order of testing the children was reversed for each day; those children who had been tested in the morning were now tested in the afternoon, and vice versa.

All the re-testing was concluded in this one week.   Almost all of the children were still available, so that there was little loss due to absence or removal.   There had been eighty-two children first tested, but some few had left or had not taken the complete course of training.

For a period of ten weeks after the completion of this re-testing these children had their regular school work, with no intelligence or educational test of any type.   Then, thirteen weeks after the original test, one examiner re-tested all of the children.   This took about three weeks.   There were still seventy-eight of the original children left.

As has been stated before, exactly similar methods were used in A and Y, except for the fact that the "coached" group was taught the correct answers to the tests in year XII as well as to the tests in years VI to X inclusive, and all groups at Y were explored through year XII in the original test, and all cases where there was the slightest hint of possible success.

The period at Y which elapsed between the second and third tests was longer than the similar period at A.   While at A this test was given just thirteen weeks after the original test, there was a period of eighteen weeks between the first and third test at Y. This was unavoidable, owing to the arrangement of the school year, and due allowance was made for the mental growth which would naturally occur in this period.

At A the test was repeated after a lapse of fifty-five weeks from the original test, just a year after the first re-test following the training.   This was conducted by the same examiner who tested the groups at A and Y for their third tests.

CHAPTER V

RESULTS

This experiment extended over a considerable period of time. Since mental age is dependent on chronological age during the first ten years of life, at least for normal children, we have here an extraneous factor influencing the amount of gain shown by the children, while we want to measure only that part of the gain due to the training alone.

It was also necessary to allow for the effect of the time between the tests upon the child's results in order to compare the results from school A with those from school Y, since the period between the tests was not the same for both.

There were two methods of making such an allowance which were considered. All results might be treated on the basis of the Intelligence Quotient found in the first test. All scores might be turned into Intelligence Quotients, and comparisons made from these scores with the scores of the re-test results. But in this investigation I was not interested in the relation between scores of this sort. My interest was in the relation between the mental age obtained in a first test and the mental age and gains therein which were obtained by later re-tests after varied courses of training. There was another way in which the value of the scores might have been expressed through the Intelligence Quotients. In the case where the period between the first test and the re-test is a year, an estimate of the possible mental growth can be made by multiplying the chronological period and the Intelligence Quotient found in the first test. Such a method has a very large chance of error, for the Intelligence Quotient is determined on the basis of one test only, and is very likely to be inaccurate for many of the cases. Rugg[1] says, "The chances are one in two

---

[1] Rugg and Colloton, "Constancy of the Stanford-Binet I. Q. as Shown by Re-tests." *Journal of Educational Psychology,* September 1921.

that an I.Q. from a single test will increase as much as six points, or decrease as much as three; that the chances are one in five that it will increase as much as twelve, or decrease as much as six; and that the chances are one in twenty that it will increase as much as eighteen or decrease as much as nine."

In order to get rid of this error due to the inaccuracy of the first test results, the most impartial method would be to say that all had had an equal gain during the period under investigation. The relationship between original success and subsequent improvement in a set task is so little explained at the present time that any other method is open to many dangers from errors made under misapprehension of the nature of this relationship. If we were to assume that all had gained equally, it would be best to say that each child gained as though he were a child progressing at the normal rate of growth; that is, a child whose I.Q. was 100 for any and each interval of time. The average Intelligence Quotients for the three groups varied less than seven points from the average Intelligence Quotient of the entire group.

This was the method adopted, when each month of chronological gain is assumed to mean a month of mental gain. By doing this two chances for error are eliminated. The personal bias of the tester is not felt, since the tendency of a tester to give more credit than another would have given does not lessen the credit for the amount actually gained by her subjects subsequently. The condition of the child at the time of the first test does not influence the amount of estimated gain. This method is both impartial and simple. It makes allowances for various disturbing factors with the least possible injury to the true scores.

The first mental age achieved by the child in the first test given in this experiment is taken as the basis for all calculations. It is not, of course, a strictly accurate measure of the child's mental ability. Rugg[2] says (p. 316): "This means that the chances are one in two that an I.Q. from a single test will increase as much as six points or decrease as much as three." But as this inaccuracy is distributed by chance, we can not clear it out of these results, since we could not give a second test to make the score a more reliable measure.

The first re-test (second test) came just three weeks later.

---

[2] "Constancy of the Stanford-Binet I. Q. as Shown by Re-tests." *Journal of Educational Psychology,* September 1921.

The effect of this period on mental age is deduced from its effect on chronological age. If the child is regarded as having gained a month, chronologically (calculating the monthly birthday nearest to the date of the test), then the three weeks is regarded as a period of one month advance. If there is no change in chronological age (as calculated to the nearest monthly birthday), the influence of this period is disregarded. In the majority of cases, one month has been added to the chronological age. Then one month is subtracted from the total number of months made on the second test, in order to make this score commensurate with the first, so far as time is concerned.

A similar process is passed by the scores of the third test (second re-test) for both A and Y. Now that the results from A and Y are translated into terms of the original scores, we can combine A and Y though the difference in length of time had made this impossible before.

With these three scores in terms of the original score, we have to take one more step to make them strictly commensurate. It was impossible to get three testers who would rate exactly alike in each situation. There is a tendency for one tester to grade a child a bit higher than another tester would grade him. While this effect is small with such well-trained testers, it is present. In ordinary work it may well be disregarded, but in this instance the results that we want are complicated by the effect of this individual difference.

There was no way of finding out how far each tester deviated from a theoretically perfect tester. Such information would have been helpful, for we could then have turned all results into results in terms of this standard. All we knew was the relation of each of the three testers to the other two. An average of the first results would not represent what each examiner should have as the approximate average of the group she tested. The groups are too varied in actual ability to make such a procedure reliable. It would be even more impossible to average the results of the first re-test, since by that time the children were definitely separated into three sub-groups by the training which they had had.

Fortunately there is one means of solving this dilemma. What we need to know is the effect of the training as measured by the results of the second test compared with those of the first, after the influence of the tester has been rendered constant. This was done by averaging the differences found in each of the three groups, and getting the average of the differences found by each tester in the two cases where the first test had been given by each of the other testers. This is summarized in Table VIII. The difference between the average for the whole group and that for the sub-group is found and the difference is subtracted algebraically from each score in the sub-group. The method is shown in Table VIIIA. These scores are used throughout in answering all questions as to the amount of learning made under any of the three procedures under investigation in this experiment.

TABLE VIII

AVERAGE DIFFERENCES OF SCORES; II-I TEST
CONTROL GROUP A

X=Average of all scores. Y=Average of scores when "a" gives first test and "b" gives second test. Z=Average of scores when "b" gives first test, and "a" gives second test.

$X = 4.04$
$X - Y = 4.04 - 3.25 = + .79 = + 1$ (in nearest unit)
$X - Z = 4.04 - 3.75 = + .29 = + 0$ (in nearest unit)

TABLE VIIIA

GIVEN SCORE IN THE THREE TESTS OF I = 70, II = 72, III = 73

It becomes under Conditions Y (Table VIII)			It becomes under Conditions Z (Table VIII)		
I	II	III	I	II	III
70	72	73	70	72	72
	(72 + 1)			(72 + 0)	

After the conclusion of this last step, the data are in a state where they can be examined for the effect of the training. This is presented in Table IX.

It is worth noting that the "control" group gains a little less than three months (2.88) of mental age in the second test, after the effect of different testers and of the time between tests has been allowed for. Rugg[3] states that the average difference (in I.Q. points) found in re-tests given by reliable investigators was 4.5. This three months' gain found in this investigation represents about three (3.09) points average I.Q., since the average chronological age of these children is 93.02 months at the first test. Nor does the "control" group gain by the second repetition

---

[3] *Op. cit.*

of the test. Their gains are almost identical in the second and third tests over the first test.

The "coached" group shows quite a different development. Both the A and the Y groups show a marked increase in the second test, and a lowering of this gain in the third test, taken after an interval of several months. In the case of the A group we find an average gain of 23.10 months—almost two years of mental age added to the child's score by the short period of less than three hours' coaching given a week before the re-test. This is startling. Enough of this instruction is potent over a period of three months to cause grave error in the estimation of mental age at that time. There is still evident a gain over the first test of 19.07 months. This is over a year and a half advance, and is almost a year and a half more than is found in the "control" group also taking their third test (16).

The Y group (having been coached on the eight tests of year XII in addition to those used at A) shows an even larger increase at the first re-test. Here is a gain of over two and a half years of mental age (31.71 months). This greater increase drops more rapidly than the smaller increase at A, for by the time of the second re-test, four months later, the average number of months gained over the results of the first test is 17.52. The children of Y have lost much more than the children at A. This is due largely to three factors, in all probability. The period between the first and third tests is three months at A, and four months at Y. At Y the summer vacation came between tests, and the children were re-tested in the fall as soon as school opened. The mental set necessary for school and test success was hardly re-established. And the time given to group coaching in the years between years VI and X inclusive is cut from almost two hours (118.62 minutes) to less than an hour and a half (88.14 minutes). Most of the loss shown by group Y is in the year XII, and the tests which show such a large extent of retention at A are not stressed so thoroughly at Y.

The "similar" group shows an interesting development. The children gain, on the average, a little over six months of mental age (6.32 months) from the practice in similar material. That is, it was possible to improve by a little more than three months the performance that this group made over what we would expect from the repetition of the test without such practice (6.32–2.88

or 3.44 months). This was done by a tester in the school room working with the children for a maximum period of eighteen hours. It is probable that a class-room teacher who knows the test, as many now do, will alter the performance of her class by as much as this during the course of a year. It would seem that comparisons of a class taught by a test-conscious teacher with a class taught by a more naïve teacher would favor the first group because of this one factor at least.

TABLE IX

RESULTS OF THREE TYPES OF TREATMENT, EXPRESSED IN AVERAGES

One Month of Mental Age is the Unit

CONTROL GROUP

	M. A. I T.	Dist. S. D.	M. A. II T	Dist. S. D.	Gain II-I	Dist. S. D.	M. A. III T	Dist. S. D.	Gain III-I	Dist. S. D.
A (25).	87.2	9.43	91.04	9.25	3.84	4.63	92.40	10.09	4.12	5.51
Y (28).	84.57	7.81	86.57	8.36	2	3.08	85.28	7.78	.71	4.41
A and Y (53).	85.81	8.70	88.68	9.26	2.88	3.93	88.64	9.61	2.86	5.59

COACHED GROUP

	M. A. I T.	Dist. S. D.	M. A. II T	Dist. S. D.	Gain II-I	Dist. S. D.	M. A. III T	Dist. S. D.	Gain III-I	Dist. S. D.
A (29).	86.66	8.09	109.76	6.65	23.10	6.19	105.72	7.18	19.07	5.84
Y (21).	88.43	6.06	121.33	8.73	31.71	7.23	105.95	10.03	17.52	9.39
A and Y (50).	87.40	7.43								

SIMILAR GROUP

	M. A. I T.	Dist. S. D.	M. A. II T	Dist. S. D.	Gain II-I	Dist. S. D.	M. A. III T	Dist. S. D.	Gain III-I	Dist. S. D.
A (24).	92.04	6.73	99.54	8.50	7.5	5.57	102.54	8.91	10.5	2.13
Y (26).	94.92	7.75	100.15	7.33	5.23	4.54	98.88	8.63	3.96	3.67
A and Y (50).	93.54	10.31	99.86	7.92	6.32	5.70	100.64	8.90	7.10	6.24
Total (153)..	88.85	8.64								

At school A, the tests were given again at the end of a year. For this group, then, we have four tests: the first one before any training was given; the second three weeks later, following the training period; the third at the end of three months; and the fourth at the end of a year.

The group which survived the changes of a year numbers seventy-one: twenty-one in the control group, twenty-eight in the coached group, and twenty-two in the similar group. This group closely resembles the original group in averages and standard deviations. That is, those children who have been lost were not the especially good or the especially poor.

An interesting development is found in the change in the standing of the three groups at the end of the year. The control
group has gained four months (4.27) more than would have been
expected at this time, had the intervening chronological year added
twelve months of mental age to the rating of each child. The
coached group has nine months (9.10) in excess, while the
"similar" group has only five months (4.73)—very little more
than the control group. The standard deviations for each group
are large, but the losses between the third and fourth tests in the
"similar" and coached groups are real losses, while the control
group remains at about the same advance as before. It may well
be that re-testing alone is as effective in raising the score of a
child in a test of this sort as is drill in correct responses to
material closely similar to the test material after a considerable
lapse of time since the drill and testing. The subject is not so
likely to feel that he knows the answers, and need pay no heed
to the conditions the tester is setting up. He may be more willing
to try unknown material, since he does not expect to have been
taught the answers. He is not hampered, as is a child from the
trained group, by partially remembered fragments that were once
successful responses. Nor is he so likely to remember incorrectly
and be satisfied without further thought. At least, the results
given in Table IXA point to some such solution as the best
explanation.

TABLE IXA

RESULTS OF TRAINING. RETESTS MADE OVER A PERIOD OF A YEAR

Test I made at the start.
Test II made three weeks after Test I.
Test III made three months after Test I.
Test IV made twelve months after Test I.

	Control Group (21)		Coached Group (28)		Similar Group (22)	
	Average	S. D. of Dist.	Average	S. D. of Dist.	Average	S. D. of Dist.
I	86.47	7.9	86.61	8.22	92.54	6.30
II	90.24	7.9	109.57	6.68	100.41	7.86
III	92.05	9.6	105.25	7.05	102.05	7.70
IV	90.74	10.03	95.71	6.83	97.27	8.47

The children at Y did not learn the tests to which they were exposed so well as did the children at A. Yet the children at A averaged 118.62 minutes per child.in the group coaching (see Appendix III) and 46.86 minutes individual instruction, while at Y each child received an average of 117.46 minutes per child for group' work, and 86.38 minutes for individual coaching. Table XII gives the comparative amounts of time spent in training. It gives rise to the question as to why the group at Y does not profit equally well by the increased range of tests. Is it due to less coaching on the simpler tests, and to more coaching-time being spent on tests which the child can not learn? Table XIII gives us the key by showing the amounts of time spent in coaching exclusive of the tests in year XII.

The group at A learns more of the tests between years VI and X inclusive. As these tests are the ones which are best remembered, the reason for the greater drop in the tests remembered by the Y group at the third test is plain. These children at Y were not so well coached on the first tests, and they forgot the tests in year XII faster than the simpler tests. A had learned these easier tests more thoroughly, and retained a larger amount of the coaching.

The percentage of the two groups learning the tests between VI and X is interesting. If all the children learned all the tests presented to them on which they had failed the first time, the average improvement of the A group would have been 16.60 tests. It is 9.53 tests, or 63 per cent of the possible improvement. At Y, the average improvement would have been 15.67, for perfect scores, and it is 7.09, or 45 per cent. This relationship is shown in terms of the tests learned by the two groups in Table XIII.

There is little relation in any group between the mental age and the amount gained in the period between tests. Table XVIII gives these correlations, all of which are small, either negatively or positively.

The gap between the groups as they were originally formed is about nine months. The differences between the averages of the sub-groups and the average of the group as a whole are given in Table X.

It brings up an interesting problem about the relative amounts learned by the "coached" group at A and the "coached" group at Y. If all the children learned all the tests presented to them on

TABLE X

COMPARISONS OF THE GROUPS AS DIVIDED PREPARATORY TO THE TRAINING
PERIOD

	Total Group	Control Group	Coached "A"	Coached "Y"	Similar
AverageMental Age.........	88.85 (153)	85.81 (53)	86.66 (29)	88.43 (21)	93.54 (50)
Deviation from Group Average..........	....	−3.04	−2.19	− .45	+4.69
r of 1st Score with M. A. Gained:					
School A...	....	− .26	+ .18	....	− .12
School Y...	....	.0	....	+ .20	− .38

which they had failed the first time, the average improvement of
the A group would have been 33.34 tests. As a matter of fact,
this group did learn on the average 23.10 tests, so that the percentage of tests learned to those in which there was an opportunity
to learn was 69.58. On following through the same attack on Y,
we find the percentage to be 57.06, including the tests of year
XII. This is worked out in Table XI.

TABLE XI

RELATION IN COACHED GROUPS OF ACTUAL TO POSSIBLE IMPROVEMENT
Mental Age—One Month Is the Unit

a	b	c	d	e
Greatest Possible Average Mental Age	Average Score in I Test	Average Gain Possible at II Test	Average Gain as Shown by II–I Test	$\frac{d}{c}$ in Per Cents
Through Year X............... (120)	A 86.66	A 33.34	A 23.10	A 69.58
Through Year XII............. (144)	Y 88.43	Y 55.57	Y 31.71	Y 57.06

TABLE XII

Time (In Minutes) Spent in Coaching

	Group Coaching				Individual Coaching			
	VI–XII		VI–X		VI–XII		VI–X	
	Total	Average	Total	Average	Total	Average	Total	Average
A........	....	....	3440	118.62 (29)	....	....	1359	46.86 (29)
Y........	2466	117.46 (21)	1851	88.14 (21)	1851	88.14 (21)	1110	52.86 (21)

TABLE XIII

Results of Coaching, in Averages

One Month Mental Age on Scale Between Years VI–X Inclusive = 1

	I Test	S. D. of Dist.	II Test	S. D. of Dist.	Gain Test II–I	S. D. of Dist.	A–Y	S. D. of Dist.
A (29)...........	26.79	7.84	48.45	5.69	21.65	6.59	2.04	9.14
Y (21)..........	28.66	5.61	48.28	6.17	19.61	6.34	......	......

RESULTS FOR THE SEPARATE TESTS

If we take up the effects of coaching on the tests themselves, measuring the gains by the numbers of children making such gains, we get a new set of results from this work. The number of children passing each of the tests the first time is shown in Table XIV. This gives us some measure of the relative difficulty of the individual tests for the groups concerned. If we now stop to consider the effects of training within the group, we have Table XV. Each group is arbitrarily divided in two, one-half being those who learned the greater number of tests throughout the series, and the other half those who learned fewer tests. Some tests are learned equally well by both halves, and may be considered as fairly easy to learn. Some tests are rather difficult to learn, as is shown by the comparatively small percentage learning them in the upper group, where the average per cent of learning is high. Those tests that are learned fairly well but that require a moderate amount of stressing are shown by low per cents in the lower group, and higher per cents in the upper group.

There are few such conclusions which can be drawn reliably between the upper and lower halves of these groups, because the groups are so small, and chance variation plays so large a part in the divisions made above.

Comparisons between the various groups are made more readily for the whole series by the use of the shorter form in Table XVI, while Table XVII endeavors to show what part of the improvement of the "similar" and "coached" groups is due to the training itself after the effect due to mere repetition (as shown in the results of the "control" group) is removed. This is done by subtracting from each test result, given in per cents, in the training groups the result, also in per cents, shown by the control groups.

TABLE XIV

NUMBER OF CHILDREN IN EACH GROUP PASSING TEST THE FIRST TRIAL

	Year VI						Year VII					
No.	1	2	3	4	5	6	1	2	3	4	5	6
Control Group (53)	52	44	53	43	53	33	52	43	39	41	30	34
Coached A... (29)	29	23	29	26	29	23	28	24	21	24	13	10
Coached Y... (21)	18	19	21	17	21	13	21	17	20	16	15	18
Similar....... (50)	49	45	50	47	50	43	50	41	43	41	42	39
Total...... (153)	148	131	153	133	153	112	151	125	123	122	100	101

	Year VIII						Year IX					
No.	1	2	3	4	5	6	1	2	3	4	5	6
Control Group (53)	11	31	17	18	13	2	3	9	22	9	4	18
Coached A... (29)	7	17	8	10	6	3	6	5	15	8	0	13
Coached Y... (21)	5	16	8	8	8	0	0	4	10	6	2	8
Similar....... (50)	18	44	25	27	26	4	10	14	29	23	11	29
Total...... (153)	41	108	58	63	53	9	19	32	76	46	17	68

	Year X						Year XII							
No.	1	2	3	4	5	6	1	2	3	4	5	6	7	8
Control Group (53)	0	2	1	1	2	6	0	1	0	0	0	1	0	0
Coached A... (29)	0	1	4	0	0	6	0	0	1	0	0	0	0	0
Coached Y... (21)	0	1	3	1	1	4	0	0	0	0	0	1	0	0
Similar....... (50)	0	3	8	5	2	5	0	0	3	0	0	7	0	1
Total...... (153)	0	7	16	7	5	21	0	1	4	0	0	9	0	1

TABLE XV
RESULTS OF TRAINING WITHIN GROUP

	Year VI						Year VII					
	1	2	3	4	5	6	1	2	3	4	5	6
					Control Group		—Upper Half					
1	100	88	x	0	x	54	100	33	0	14	57	25
2	1	8	0	5	0	13	1	6	10	7	14	8
					Control Group		—Lower Half					
1	x	100	x	80	x	57	x	50	–	0	44	0
2	0	1	0	5	0	7	0	4	4	5	9	11
					Control Group		—Total					
1	100	89	x	40	x	55	100	40	–	8	52	11
2	1	9	0	10	0	20	1	10	14	12	23	19
					A—Coached Group		—Upper Half					
1	x	100	x	100	x	100	100	100	0	100	100	60
2	0	4	0	2	0	4	1	3	4	2	9	10
					A—Coached Group		—Lower Half					
1	x	100	x	100	x	100	x	100	25	0	100	44
2	0	2	0	1	0	2	0	2	4	3	7	9
					A—Coached Group		—Total					
1	x	100	x	100	x	100	100	100	13	40	100	53
2	0	6	0	3	0	6	1	5	8	5	16	19
					Y—Coached Group		—Upper Half					
1	0	100	x	100	x	100	x	100	0	100	100	100
2	2	2	0	2	0	4	0	1	1	2	4	1
					Y—Coached Group		—Lower Half					
1	100	x	x	50	x	75	x	67	–	67	–	50
2	1	0	0	2	0	4	0	3	0	3	2	2
					Y—Coached Group		—Total					
1	33	100	x	75	x	88	x	75	–	80	50	67
2	3	2	0	4	0	8	0	4	1	5	6	3
					Similar Group		—Upper Half					
1	100	66	x	0	x	100	x	17	0	33	100	38
2	1	3	0	1	0	4	0	6	3	6	5	8
					Similar Group		—Lower Half					
1	–	50	x	–	–	33	x	67	50	33	0	–
2	0	2	0	2	0	3	0	3	4	3	3	3
					Similar Group		—Total					
1	–	60	x	–	–	71	x	33	29	33	63	–
2	1	5	0	3	0	7	0	9	7	9	8	11

1. $\dfrac{\text{Number passing II Test}}{\text{Number failing I Test}}$ expressed in per cent.
2. Number who failed the test the first time.
x. No chance for improvement.
—. A minus per cent.

TABLE XV—*Continued*

	Year VIII						Year IX					
	1	2	3	4	5	6	1	2	3	4	5	6
					Control Group	—Upper Half						
1	5	57	5	13	11	4	8	5	20	4	4	53
2	19	14	19	16	19	25	25	22	20	23	24	17
					Control Group	—Lower Half						
1	13	–	6	0	5	0	–	18	–	5	8	11
2	23	8	17	19	21	26	25	22	11	21	25	18
					Control Group	—Total						
1	10	32	6	6	8	2	2	11	3	5	6	31
2	42	22	36	35	40	51	50	44	31	44	49	35
					A—Coached Group	—Upper Half						
1	100	100	100	100	92	54	42	77	100	36	93	88
2	11	8	12	11	13	13	12	13	8	11	14	8
					A—Coached Group	—Lower Half						
1	82	75	89	88	60	46	9	55	83	50	87	63
2	11	4	8	9	10	13	11	11	6	10	15	8
					A—Coached Group	—Total						
1	91	92	95	95	78	50	26	67	93	43	90	75
2	22	12	21	19	23	26	23	24	14	21	29	16
					Y—Coached Group	—Upper Half						
1	100	100	100	100	71	10	10	50	83	86	89	83
2	7	3	7	8	7	10	10	8	6	7	9	6
					Y—Coached Group	—Lower Half						
1	100	50	83	100	67	18	27	89	80	25	90	86
2	9	2	6	5	6	11	11	9	5	8	10	7
					Y—Coached Group	—Total						
1	100	80	92	100	69	14	19	71	82	53	89	85
2	16	5	13	13	13	21	21	17	11	15	19	13
					Similar Group	—Upper Half						
1	72	100	33	55	–	0	22	35	36	53	14	0
2	18	3	12	11	13	23	18	17	11	15	21	10
					Similar Group	—Lower Half						
1	36	–	–	42	–	4	18	42	20	–	–	27
2	14	3	13	12	11	23	22	19	10	12	18	11
					Similar Group	—Total						
1	56	33	12	46	–	2	20	39	29	7	5	14
2	32	6	25	23	24	46	40	36	21	27	39	21

TABLE XV—*Concluded*

	\multicolumn{6}{Year X}						\multicolumn{8}{Year XII}							

	1	2	3	4	5	6	1	2	3	4	5	6	7	8
			Control	Group		—Upper	Half							
1	0	4	23	8	12	12	0	0	4	0	4	0	4	0
2	26	25	26	25	25	25	26	26	26	26	26	26	26	26
			Control	Group		—Lower	Half							
1	0	4	11	15	0	5	0	–	4	0	0	0	0	0
2	27	26	26	27	26	22	27	26	27	27	27	26	27	27
			Control	Group		—Total								
1	0	4	17	11	6	8	0	–	4	0	2	0	2	0
2	53	51	52	52	51	47	53	52	53	53	53	52	53	53
			A—Coached	Group		—Upper	Half							
1	0	78	78	71	64	33	0	0	54	0	0	14	0	0
2	14	14	14	14	14	12	14	14	13	14	14	14	14	14
			A—Coached	Group		—Lower	Half							
1	7	57	100	67	47	18	0	0	47	0	0	7	0	7
2	15	14	11	15	15	11	15	15	15	15	15	15	15	15
			A—Coached	Group		—Total								
1	3	68	88	69	55	26	0	0	50	0	0	10	0	0
2	29	28	25	29	29	23	29	29	28	29	29	29	29	29
			Y—Coached	Group		—Upper	Half							
1	0	80	90	90	80	0	0	20	90	90	70	40	50	90
2	10	10	10	10	10	8	10	10	10	10	10	10	10	10
			Y—Coached	Group		—Lower	Half							
1	9	60	75	90	50	33	0	0	91	82	36	10	18	64
2	11	10	8	10	10	9	11	11	11	11	11	10	11	11
			Y—Coached	Group		—Total								
1	5	70	83	90	65	17	0	9	91	86	52	25	33	76
2	21	20	18	20	20	17	21	21	21	21	21	20	21	21
			Similar	Group		—Upper	Half							
1	0	12	55	26	0	30	0	0	72	0	4	22	0	0
2	25	25	22	23	24	23	25	25	25	25	25	23	25	24
			Similar	Group		—Lower	Half							
1	0	5	60	18	8	18	0	0	13	0	0	5	0	0
2	25	22	20	22	24	22	25	25	22	25	25	20	25	25
			Similar	Group		—Total								
1	0	9	57	22	4	24	0	0	43	0	2	14	0	0
2	50	47	42	45	48	45	50	50	47	50	50	43	50	49

TABLE XVI

Per Cent Learned in Each Group

100 *Per cent = Complete success for all those failing the test on first trial.*
X = No chances to learn.

	Year VI							Year VII					
	1	2	3	4	5	6		1	2	3	4	5	6
Control Group	100	89	X	40	X	55		100	40	0	8	52	11
A—Coached Group	X	100	X	100	X	100		100	100	13	40	100	53
Y—Coached Group	33	100	X	75	X	88		X	75	0	80	50	67
Similar Group	0	60	X	0	X	71		X	33	29	33	63	0

	Year VIII							Year IX					
	1	2	3	4	5	6		1	2	3	4	5	6
Control Group	10	32	6	6	8	2		2	11	3	5	6	31
A—Coached Group	91	92	95	95	78	50		26	67	93	43	90	75
Y—Coached Group	100	80	92	100	69	14		19	71	82	53	89	85
Similar Group	56	33	12	46	0	2		20	39	29	7	5	14

	Year X							Year XII							
	1	2	3	4	5	6		1	2	3	4	5	6	7	8
Control Group	0	4	17	11	6	8		0	0	4	0	2	0	2	0
A—Coached Group	3	68	88	69	55	26		0	0	50	0	0	10	0	0
Y—Coached Group	5	70	83	90	65	17		0	9	91	86	52	25	33	76
Similar Group	0	9	57	22	4	24		0	0	43	0	2	14	0	0

Results

39

TABLE XVII

COMPARATIVE TABLE OF PERCENTAGES OF CHILDREN LEARNING A TEST
AFTER FAILURE IN FIRST TEST

a = Cases learning test.   () = Number failing at first trial.

$$b = \frac{\text{Number passing II Test}}{\text{Number failing I Test}} \text{ expressed in per cent.}$$

X = 0 *learned, with zero chances to learn.*

Test	Control (53)	Coach School A (29)	Coach School Y (21)	Similar (50)
VI 1				
a	1 (1)	X	1 (3)	−1 (1)
b	100		33	−100
VI 2				
a	8 (9)	6 (6)	2 (2)	3 (5)
b	89	100	100	60
VI 3				
a	X	X	X	X
b				
VI 4				
a	4 (10)	3 (3)	3 (4)	−1 (3)
b	40	100	75	−33
VI 5				
a	X	X	X	X
b				
VI 6				
a	11 (20)	6 (6)	7 (8)	5 (7)
b	55	100	88	71
VII 1				
a	1 (1)	1 (1)	X	X
b	100	100		
VII 2				
a	4 (10)	5 (5)	3 (4)	3 (9)
b	40	100	75	33
VII 3				
a	−3 (14)	1 (8)	−2 (1)	2 (7)
b	−26	13	−200	29
VII 4				
a	1 (12)	2 (5)	4 (5)	3 (9)
b	8	40	80	33
VII 5				
a	12 (23)	16 (16)	3 (6)	5 (8)
b	52	100	50	63
VII 6				
a	2 (19)	10 (19)	2 (3)	−2 (11)
b	11	53	67	−18

TABLE XVII—*Continued*

	Control	Coached A	Coached Y	Similar
VIII 1				
a............	4 (42)	20 (22)	16 (16)	18 (32)
b............	10	91	100	56
VIII 2				
a............	7 (22)	11 (12)	4 (5)	2 (6)
b............	32	92	80	33
VIII 3				
a............	2 (36)	20 (21)	12 (13)	3 (25)
b............	6	95	92	12
VIII 4				
a............	2 (35)	18 (19)	13 (13)	11 (23)
b............	6	95	100	46
VIII 5				
a............	3 (40)	18 (23)	9 (13)	−4 (24)
b............	8	78	69	−16
VIII 6				
a............	1 (51)	13 (26)	3 (21)	1 (46)
b............	2	50	14	2
IX 1				
a............	1 (50)	6 (23)	4 (21)	8 (40)
b............	2	26	19	20
IX 2				
a............	5 (44)	16 (24)	12 (17)	14 (36)
b............	11	67	71	39
IX 3				
a............	1 (31)	13 (14)	9 (11)	6 (21)
b............	3	93	82	29
IX 4				
a............	2 (44)	9 (21)	8 (15)	2 (27)
b............	5	43	53	7
IX 5				
a............	3 (49)	26 (29)	17 (19)	2 (39)
b............	6	90	89	5
IX 6				
a............	11 (35)	12 (16)	11 (13)	3 (21)
b............	31	75	85	14

TABLE XVII—*Concluded*

	Control	Coached A	Coached Y	Similar
X 1				
a............	0 (53)	1 (29)	1 (21)	0 (50)
b............	0	3	5	0
X 2				
a............	2 (51)	19 (28)	14 (20)	4 (47)
b............	4	68	70	9
X 3				
a............	9 (52)	22 (25)	15 (18)	24 (42)
b............	17	88	83	57
X 4				
a............	6 (52)	20 (29)	18 (20)	10 (45)
b............	11	69	90	22
X 5				
a............	3 (51)	16 (29)	13 (20)	2 (48)
b............	6	55	65	4
X 6				
a............	4 (47)	6 (23)	3 (17)	11 (45)
b............	8	26	17	24
XII 1				
a...........	0 (53)	0 (29)	0 (21)	0 (50)
b...........	0	0	0	0
XII 2				
a...........	−1 (52)	0 (29)	2 (21)	0 (50)
b...........	−2	0	9	0
XII 3				
a...........	2 (53)	14 (28)	19 (21)	21 (47)
b...........	4	50	91	43
XII 4				
a...........	0 (53)	0 (29)	18 (21)	0 (50)
b...........	0	0	86	0
XII 5				
a...........	1 (53)	0 (29)	11 (21)	1 (50)
b...........	2	0	52	2
XII 6				
a...........	0 (52)	3 (29)	5 (20)	6 (43)
b...........	0	10	25	14
XII 7				
a...........	1 (53)	0 (29)	7 (21)	0 (50)
b...........	2	0	33	0
XII 8				
a...........	0 (53)	0 (29)	16 (21)	0 (49)
b...........	0	0	76	0

TABLE XVIII

CORRELATIONS OF SCORES AND GAINS

CONTROL GROUP

	II	III	IV	Gain II-I	Gain III-I	Gain IV-I
Control School A						
I..........	86	80	75	− 26	− 13	− 07
Gain II-I.......					70	02
Gain III-I......						30
Control School Y						
I..........	92	60		0	− 33	
Gain II-I.......					35	
Gain III-I......						
Combined Schools						
A and Y						
I..........	89	75		− 12	− 13	
Gain II-I.......					46	
Gain III-I......						

COACHED GROUP

	II	III	IV	Gain II-I	Gain III-I	Gain IV-I
Coached School A						
I..........	64	70	68	18	− 51	− 60
Gain II-I.......					81	44
Gain III-I......						63
Coached School Y						
I..........	55	43		20	− 27	
Gain II-I.......					48	
Gain III-I......						
Combined Schools						
A and Y						
I..........	53	53				
Gain II-I.......						
Gain III-I......						

TABLE XVIII—*Concluded*

CORRELATIONS OF SCORES AND GAINS

SIMILAR GROUP

	II	III	IV	Gain II-I	Gain III-I	Gain IV-I
Similar School A						
I..............	78	63	53	− 28	− 15	− 62
Gain II-I.......					58	58
Gain III-I......						80
Similar School Y						
I..............	82	90		− 38	− 02	
Gain II-I.......					− 07	
Gain III-I......						
Combined Schools A and Y						
I..............	79	71		− 36	− 21	
Gain II-I.......					49	
Gain III-I......						

CHAPTER VI

CONCLUSIONS

1. Direct coaching on the material of the tests is extremely effective, even when the time given to the coaching is small.
2. The effect of such direct coaching persists to a large degree for a period of three or four months, at least.
3. The effects of direct coaching are not highly correlated with the mental ages measured by the first giving of the test.
4. Comparisons between coached and uncoached children are not possible on the basis of the tests in which coaching has been given to the first group.
5. Indirect coaching, or training in work similar to the material of the tests, is also effective, though to a much smaller degree. This effect is serious enough to be considered.
6. The effect of such indirect coaching persists to a large degree for a period of three or four months, at least.
7. The effects of this indirect coaching are correlated negatively to a slight degree with the Mental Age measured by the first giving of the test.
8. Comparisons between children in a group where the teacher has not known the Binet tests and children whose teacher is a believer in the value of the tests, will be slightly unfair to the first group. A great many teachers who feel that the tests are effective, feel also that they will make good training material for their classes and so are likely to use this material directly, or indirectly.
9. Several alternative forms of the individual examination series are needed, in order to measure intelligence with as little disturbance as possible from coaching, conscious or unconscious.
10. An effort should be made to find tests which are non-coachable. Since many tests of this type do not differentiate well, it would be advisable to give a practice period on material used in intelligence tests, and make comparisons between children on the basis of subsequent testing.

11. The control group gains considerably from the repetition of the test. Continued testing gives a child an undue advantage over a child who has never had the test before.
12. The training which gave the coached and "similar" groups an initial advantage, seems at the end of the year to have lowered their gains as compared with the gains of the control group. Such an effect is probably due partly to the memory of mistakes, and partly to inaccurate memory of the coached responses.
13. None of these results gives us material for deciding the nature of intelligence. They do point out some dangers from which we must safeguard future tests of intelligence.
14. Since the effect of closely similar training is so slight after the lapse of a year, it seems probable that the differences in the educative ability of various school systems have little differentiating effect on the standing of their pupils in intelligence examinations.

APPENDIX I

TABLE XIX

COMPLETE TABLE OF RESULTS

The Results are Equaled to the First Teet (p. 25) but the Influence of the Tester has not been Removed

Coached Group A

	Chronological Age	Mental Ages			
		I	II	III	IV
1	7–2	72	97	96	88
2	7–2	72	104	93	85
3	9–1	72	96	89	84
4	8–3	76	114	103	83
5	7–9	78	103	96	91
6	9	80	103	95	85
7	9	81	111	105	95
8	7–8	82	109	109	103
9	8–6	84	104	101	92
10	8–1	84	104	108	93
11	8–2	84	109	104	93
12	7–3	86	116	114	107
13	7–3	86	107	100	99
14	8–5	86	117	105	96
15	9–5	87	110	109	95
16	8–4	88	111	109	Inc.
17	7–11	88	108	106	95
18	10	88	112	108	97
19	7–11	89	114	109	97
20	7–8	90	114	105	103
21	9–1	90	119	115	97
22	10–3	90	117	109	102
23	8–7	92	118	113	103
24	7–2	92	107	102	85
25	8–3	96	111	110	102
26	10–11	96	106	102	94
27	7–11	98	116	108	110
28	8–5	104	109	112	103
29	9	102	117	121	103

TABLE XIX—*Continued*

COACHED GROUP Y

	Chronological Age	Mental Ages			
		I	II	III	IV
1	7–8	80	126	115	
2	7–8	82	114	100	
3	7–11	82	120	101	
4	7–10	84	115	95	
5	7–7	84	123	117	
6	7–4	84	96	88	
7	8–7	86	121	110	
8	7–9	86	138	110	
9	8–3	86	124	109	
10	7–5	86	127	104	
11	7–7	86	111	88	
12	7–9	88	104	94	
13	7–8	88	129	109	
14	8–4	88	116	107	
15	7–8	88	125	109	
16	7–2	92	120	105	
17	6–10	92	110	116	
18	7–1	92	117	107	
19	6–11	98	129	117	
20	7–11	99	112	95	
21	8–3	106	135	129	

SIMILAR GROUP

	Chronological Age	Mental Ages			
		I	II	III	IV
1 A 1	8–6	76	98	93	90
2 A 2	7–5	78	79	87	Inc.
3 Y 1	7–4	80	83	89	
4 Y 2	7–9	82	91	84	
5 A 3	8–5	84	93	96	87
6 A 4	6–10	84	81	85	83
7 A 5	7–8	86	98	101	102
8 Y 3	7–11	86	91	86	
9 Y 4	7–10	88	95	97	
10 A 6	6–10	88	100	100	96

TABLE XIX—*Continund*

SIMILAR GROUP—*Concluded*

	Chronological Age	Mental Ages			
		I	II	III	IV
11 A 7..........	7–2	88	94	104	91
12 Y 5..........	7–1	88	99	86	
13 A 8..........	7–3	88	95	90	91
14 Y 6..........	7–2	90	95	98	
15 Y 7..........	8	90	93	96	
16 Y 8..........	8–2	90	94	93	
17 Y 9..........	7–6	90	97	93	
18 Y 10..........	7–11	91	96	97	
19 A 9..........	8–6	92	110	113	104
20 Y 11..........	6–10	92	94	87	
21 A 10..........	10–7	92	100	104	91
22 A 11..........	7–2	92	93	101	95
23 Y 12..........	7–7	93	92	99	
24 A 12..........	6–10	94	107	117	113
25 A 13..........	8–7	94	95	105	91
26 Y 13..........	7–10	94	96	94	
27 A 14..........	8–10	94	97	96	95
28 Y 14..........	8–4	94	102	98	
29 A 15..........	8–1	95	101	107	Inc.
30 Y 15..........	7	96	100	99	
31 A 16..........	7–5	96	107	110	100
32 A 17..........	7–7	96	102	106	94
33 A 18..........	7–8	96	116	116	110
34 A 19..........	7–7	96	107	107	103
35 Y 16..........	6–11	98	102	100	
36 A 20..........	8	98	104	104	99
37 Y 17..........	7	98	116	108	
38 A 21..........	13–6	98	101	89	85
39 Y 18..........	8	99	105	102	
40 Y 19..........	7–7	100	106	100	
41 A 22..........	8	100	99	106	99
42 Y 20..........	7–7	100	103	103	
43 Y 21..........	6–5	100	97	108	
44 Y 22..........	7–7	101	118	106	
45 A 23..........	7–7	101	103	109	108
46 Y 23..........	7–4	101	115	111	
47 Y 24..........	6–10	103	104	105	
48 A 24..........	6–9	103	110	115	113
49 Y 25..........	7–3	108	117	113	
50 Y 26..........	7–7	116	108	119	

TABLE XIX—*Continued*

CONTROL GROUP

	Chronological Age	Mental Ages			
		I	II	III	IV
1 Y 1..........	7–4	70	77	72	
2 A 1..........	8–3	70	81	83	78
3 Y 2..........	8–5	72	73	78	
4 Y 3..........	7–2	74	71	73	
5 A 2..........	7–5	76	86	83	83
6 Y 4..........	7	76	73	76	
7 Y 5..........	7–8	78	79	86	
8 Y 6..........	7–2	78	79	74	
9 A 3..........	9	78	82	83	78
10 Y 7..........	7–8	78	81	81	
11 A 4..........	6–3	78	87	85	Inc.
12 Y 8..........	7–4	79	84	82	
13 A 5..........	7–1	79	83	87	80
14 Y 9..........	7–5	80	77	77	
15 A 6..........	9–10	80	94	85	84
16 Y 10..........	7–5	80	91	85	
17 Y 11..........	7–1	80	81	85	
18 A 7..........	6–11	80	89	83	Inc.
19 A 8..........	7–3	80	82	83	82
20 Y 12..........	7–7	80	81	78	
21 A 9..........	7–2	82	85	89	95
22 Y 13..........	7–8	82	81	85	
23 Y 14..........	6–10	82	81	73	
24 A 10..........	8	82	86	91	91
25 Y 15..........	7–6	84	85	95	
26 A 11..........	9–1	84	88	83	79
27 A 12..........	9–3	86	101	96	89
28 Y 16..........	6–5	86	94	89	
29 Y 17..........		86	85	87	
30 A 13..........	9–6	86	87	85	87
31 A 14..........	6–2	87	80	87	82
32 A 15..........	9–5	88	93	91	93
33 A 16..........	7–8	88	95	93	95
34 Y 18..........	7	88	95	92	
35 Y 19..........	7–7	90	97	91	
36 Y 20..........	8–4	90	97	91	
37 A 17..........	8–1	92	96	97	96
38 Y 21..........	7	92	89	92	
39 A 18..........	7–5	92	86	91	117

TABLE XIX—*Concluded*

CONTROL GROUP—*Concluded*

	Chronological Age	Mental Ages			
		I	II	III	IV
40 Y 22..........	7–2	92	105	90	
41 A 19..........	7–6	92	94	95	Inc.
42 Y 23..........	7–10	92	87	89	
43 A 20..........	7–3	94	95	101	105
44 A 21..........	9–5	94	104	105	95
45 Y 24..........	7–6	94	97	92	
46 Y 25..........	7–5	94	89	87	
47 Y 26..........	7–8	94	90	88	
48 A 22..........	6–8	96	97	105	98
49 Y 27..........	6–10	98	107	102	
50 Y 28..........	7–4	99	97	98	
51 A 23..........	9–2	100	100	93	90
52 A 24..........	9–11	102	108	122	109
53 A 25..........	10–1	114	112	114	Inc.

APPENDIX II

MATERIAL FOR TRAINING THE "SIMILAR" GROUP

Test 8. The pictures used for description by the child were about simple childish games and activities with considerable action in each one. An attempt was made to get as much interpretation as was possible from the group.

Poullson, Emilie, and Smith, Eleanor, *Songs of a Little Child's Day.* Milton Bradley Company. Copyright, 1910.

Test 10. This test is based on the test used by Dr. Kuhlmann in the eight-year group, called "Folding a Square of Paper Five Times."[1]

Tests 23 and 24. These tests were adapted from Pintner's Scale of Performance Tests.

Test 18. The vocabulary given to the children for group definition was based on E. L. Thorndike's *Teacher's Word Book* (Teachers College, Columbia University, 1921) following the suggestion of Dr. R. Pintner. Words were selected from the list having the same frequency of use as the first twenty words in the Terman Vocabulary, first list. From among the words so selected three were chosen for each word in the Terman Vocabulary. These three were as nearly like the original as was possible in general meaning, similar part of speech, and the words were root words in the cases where it was possible to get such words. This procedure was used since it was impossible to secure in New York a copy of the dictionary used by Terman in forming his original list.

Test 26. The first half of this test is based on the test used by Dr. Kuhlmann in the ten-year group called "Detection of Absurdities in Absurd Statements."[2]

Throughout, the training depends largely on the Stanford Revision of the Binet-Simon Tests for its suggestions and basis of development.

FORM I OF "SIMILAR" TRAINING MATERIAL

Have you all sharp pencils?

We are going to have some games and questions to-day. They are like the games that most of you have been trying for

---

[1] Kuhlmann, F., *A Handbook of Mental Tests.* Warwick and York, 1922. See page 116.

[2] *Op. cit.,* p. 125.

the last week. This time we are going to find out how well all of you can do these.

Some of these games will be very easy for you, and some will be harder. I want you to try everything. When you finish we will do them together.

Have you any questions?

First write your name on this first page down near the bottom. Under your name write one, for this is the first time you have had these games. (Varied to two, and three, for the later trials.)

If you can not spell any word, just try it, and spell as well as you can.

When you finish any of these games, sit back, and wait for me to tell you what to do next.

TEST 1

Directions

Do you see these figures? (A cardboard with the figures enlarged is shown the class.)

On the first one on your paper put a cross (cross illustrated on the board) on the left side of the figure. On the second one, put across on the right side of the figure. On the third one, put a cross on the right side of the figure. On the fourth one, put a cross on the left side of the figure. On the fifth one, put a cross on the right side of the figure.

Form

1 a.

A cardboard containing enlarged figures like those on the child's sheet.

Answer

If four of the five are correctly checked, the answer is considered correct.

TEST 2

Directions

Take off the clip. Put it on your desk. Turn the page like this. (The directions for page turning are repeated where necessary.)

There is something wrong with this face. It is not all there.

Part of it is left out. Look carefully and tell me what part of
the face is not there. Put the name of what is not there beside 1, here (pointing to a sheet held in front of the experimenter).
There is something wrong with this face. It is not all there.
Part of it is left out. Look carefully and tell me what part of
the face is not there. Put the name of what is not there beside
2, here (pointing to a sheet held in front of the experimenter).
There is something wrong with this face. It is not all there.
Part of it is left out. Look carefully and tell me what part of
the face is not there. Put the name of what is not there beside 3,
here (pointing to a sheet held in front of the experimenter).
There is something wrong with this face. It is not all there.
Part of it is left out. Look carefully and tell me what part of
the face is not there. Put the name of what is not there beside
4, here (pointing to a sheet held in front of the experimenter).

Form

2 a.

1.
2.
3.
4.

Four cardboard sheets each with a large drawing of a human
face with some part left out.

Answer

Three must be correctly answered.
1. Mouth   2. Hair   3. Eyebrow   4. Nose.

TEST 3

Directions

Where you see all of these circles, put crosses in fourteen
of them.

Form

3 a.

OOOOOOOOOOOOOOOOOOOOOO

Answer

Fourteen circles crossed out.

TEST 4

Directions

Now read what it says below the circles. (Experimenter reads the first half.) Put a cross in front of the answer that you think is right.

Now read what it says just below that. (Experimenter reads the second half.) Put a cross in front of the answer that you think is right.

Form

4 a.

What's the thing for you to do when you burn your hand?

Call the police

Go outdoors to play tag

Ask some one to help you fix it

Go to sleep

What's the thing for you to do when you break your pencil in school?

Go to the store to buy a new one

Sit back and fold your hands

Ask the janitor to sharpen it

Sharpen your pencil

Answer

Both must be correctly answered.
1. A cross in the square in front of "Ask some one to help you fix it."
2. A cross in the square in front of "Sharpen your pencil."

TEST 5

Directions
1. What is this? (A dollar bill.) Write the name after one here at the top of the page. (Experimenter shows the place.)
2. What is this? (A two-cent stamp.) Write the name after two, here. (Experimenter shows the place.)
3. What is this? (A calling card.) Write the name after three, here. (Experimenter shows the place.)

4. What is this? (An envelope.) Write the name after four, here. (Experimenter shows the place.)

Form

5.

What is this?
1.
2.
3.
4.

Answer
Three must be correctly answered.
1. A dollar.
2. A stamp (two-cent stamp).
3. A card (a calling card).
4. An envelope.

Test 6

Directions
I am going to read you a sentence, and after I am through I want you to write it just as I read it. Write it here where it says one. Do you understand? Listen carefully and be sure to write exactly what I say. "The man ran fast. His little dog ran with him."

Now listen to what I read. Write this after two, right here. Listen carefully. "Boys can play ball at home. They like to throw the ball."

Now listen to what I read. Write this after three, right here. Listen carefully. "Jane has many dolls. She likes to give them a ride."

Form

6.

1.
2.
3.

Answer
Of the seven ideas in each sentence, at least five must be reported for each of two sentences.

TEST 7

Directions

How many toes have you on one foot? Write the answer after one, here.

How many toes have you on the other foot? Write the answer after two, here.

How many toes have you on both feet? Write the answer just below the number two, here.

Form

Owing to a mistake in setting up the material only 1 and 2 were printed, while 3 was omitted. This made necessary the slightly awkward directions above.

7.

1.

2.

Answer

Five, five, and ten are the correct answers. Four, four and eight accepted for fingers (see Terman, VII–1) are not valid here.

TEST 8

Directions

Tell me what this picture is about. What is this a picture of? Write what you think it is about, here after one.

(The experimenter shows the pictures already referred to at the beginning of this section so that each child may see the picture clearly.)

Tell me what this picture is about. What is this a picture of? Write what you think it is about, here after two.

Tell me what this picture is about. What is this a picture of? Write what you think it is about, here after three.

Form

8.

1.

2.

3.

Answer

A very simple answer is accepted, since it is difficult for children of this group to express themselves in writing.

1. The baby is giving the Mother flowers.
2. The boy is playing with the baby.
3. The baby is looking at the rain.

TEST 9

Directions

I am going to read you some letters, and when I am through, I want you to write them just as I read them. Write them here, after one. E-H-B-G-I. (A card is shown for five seconds, and the letters on the card are read to the children by the experimenter.) Write these, after two. B-F-D-A-C. Write these, after three. I-D-C-B-G.

Form

9.

1.
2.
3.

Answer

Two of the three must be correctly written.

TEST 10

Directions

Here on your desk is a sheet of paper. I want you to fold it just as I fold this large sheet. Watch me until I am through.

(The experimenter, following Kuhlmann's directions[3] holds the large square of paper just in front of him, and folds the upper right corner of the square onto a cross made in the center of the sheet. Then he folds the lower edge onto the center, so that the right half of this edge will meet the edge of the part folded first. Then he folds the upper left corner onto the cross at the center as in the first folding. Then he folds the corner at the top onto the lower left corner, making a rectangular piece with a truncated upper corner.)

Now you make one just like this.

Form

A square of paper, five by five inches, is on the desk of each child. The center of the sheet is marked.

Answer

Four of the five folds must be correctly made.

TEST 11

Directions

What is the difference between a man and a boy? Write the difference here, after one.

---

[3] Kuhlmann, F., *A Handbook of Mental Tests,* p. 116.

What is the difference between sugar and salt? Write the difference here, after two.

What is the difference between day and night? Write the difference here, after three.

Form

11.

1.

2.

3.

Answer

Two of three must be correct.

1. Differences in size or age accepted.
2. Differences in taste or use accepted.
3. Differences in light or use accepted.

TEST 12

Directions

Here under one make one exactly like this. (The experimenter holds up a large card with a large rectangle on it.)

Here under two make one exactly like this.

Here under three make one exactly like this.

Put a cross under the one which is best, the one that is just like this.

Form

12.

1.   2.   3.

Answer

Two rectangles with comparable dimensions and clearly drawn angles.

TEST 13

Directions

I lost my pocketbook in this pond. (Experimenter shows a large copy of the pond on the child's paper.) I can see through the water to the bottom of the pond. But I don't know in what part of the pond the pocketbook is. All I know is that the pocketbook is lost somewhere in the pond. Here is a boat in which I can row to look for my pocketbook. Now, take your pencil, and mark how you would row the boat so as to be sure not to miss the pocketbook. Begin at the boat, and show me where you would row the boat.

Form

13 a.

Answer

The drawing must approach the circular type, going in and in; some following of the pond's outline is expected.

TEST 14

Directions

You can count to 100 by 5's, can't you? Now down here, I want you to count backwards for me from 100 to 5. I want you to count clear backwards from 100 to 5 like this, 100-95-90, and clear on down to 5. Now go ahead, and write it here.

Form

14 a.

Answer

One error permitted.

TEST 15

Directions

Read what it says. (Experimenter reads the first half.) Put a cross in front of the answer that you think is right. Now read what it says just below that. (Experimenter reads the second half.) Put a cross in front of the answer that you think is right.

Form
15 a.

What's the thing for you to do when you have hurt your friend's cat?

	Be more careful
	Throw the cat in the river
	Go to the circus
	Tell the fireman

What's the thing for you to do when you know your mother needs you to help her?

	Keep on playing
	Go home and eat some bread
	Run down the hill
	Go home and help her

Answer
   Both must be correctly answered.
1. A cross in the square in front of "Be more careful."
2. A cross in the square in front of "Go home and help her."

Test 16
Directions
   1. Name something that is like a potato. Write the answer here, after one.
   2. Name something that is like a dog. Write the answer here, after two.
   3. Name something that is like a man. Write the answer here, after three.

Form
16 a.
   1.
   2.
   3.

Answer

Two must be correctly answered.

1. A vegetable, or some object comparing with potato in general roundness.
2. An animal of the domestic type, or a wild dog-like animal.
3. Some other member of the human family.

TEST 17

Directions

1. What animal do we have that gives us milk? Write the answer here, after one.
2. What thing do we live in, that keeps us warm and dry. Write the answer here, after two.
3. What thing do we have that comes from trees, and burns in the fire?
4. What animal do we have to play with, that keeps us safe?

Form

17.

1.
2.
3.
4.

Answer

Three must be correctly answered.

1. Cows.   2. Houses.   3. Wood.   4. Dogs.

TEST 18

Directions

I want to find out how many words you know. Class stand. When I say a word, you raise your hand, and I shall ask you to tell me what that word means.

1. Stocking.
2. Groan.
3. Lease.
4. Target.
5. Riddle.
6. Minute.
7. Date.
8. Normal.
9. Lumber.
10. Preach.
11. Pint.
12. Somewhere.
13. Rare.
14. Cargo.
15. Canoe.
16. Credit.
17. Romp.
18. Cunning.
19. Muffle.
20. Orphan.

Form

There was none needed for this question. The printed form was disregarded in practice.

Answer

The correct answer was supplied by some child, or by the experimenter in some few cases, and the class repeated the answer chosen in chorus, twice.

TEST 19

Directions

  a. When does Christmas come?   Write the answer here after "a."

  b. What time of the year is Easter?   Write the answer here after "b."

  c. When is your birthday?   Write the answer here after "c."

  d. When do you have a long vacation?   Write the answer here after "d."

Form

19.

  a.

  b.

  c.

  d.

Answer

Three must be correct.

a. December.

b. Spring.

c. The month is named.

d. Summer.

TEST 20

Directions

  You are to mark these figures here.   (The experimenter holds up a large sheet with these figures enlarged.)   Put 1 under the largest, put 2 under the next largest, 3 under the next largest, 4 under the next largest and 5 under the smallest.   Remember now, put 1 under the biggest, 2 under the next biggest, and 3 under the next littler and 4 under the next littler and 5 under the littlest.   Go ahead.

Form

20 a.

Answer

One error is permitted.

5-3-4-1-2.

TEST 21

Directions

I took ten cents to the store, and came home with four cents. How much did I spend? Write the answer here, after one.

I took twenty-five cents, and came back with two cents. How much did I spend? Write the answer here, after two.

I took fifteen cents, and came back with four cents. How much did I spend? Write the answer here, after three.

Form

21 a.

1.

2.

3.

Answer

Two of the three must be correctly answered.

1. Six cents.
2. Twenty-three cents.
3. Eleven cents.

TEST 22

Directions

I am going to read you some letters again, but this time I want you to write them backwards. For example, if I should read a-b-c-d, you would write d-c-b-a. Do you understand?

After 1, write these letters backwards, F-E-B-G. (The experimenter holds up a card with these letters on it.)

After 2, write these letters backwards, D-I-F-H. (The experimenter holds up a card with these letters on it.)

After 3, write these letters backwards, A-C-B-H. (The experimenter holds up a card with these letters on it.)

Form

22 a.

1.
2.
3.

Answer
Two of the three must be correctly answered.

TEST 23

Directions
You know what a word is, of course. Now I am going to give you some letters, and you must make up three words that have these letters in them. Make three words out of these letters. (The experimenter holds up a card with the letters on it.) A-E-I-R-L-P. Write them here after 1, after 2, after 3.

Form

23.

1.
2.
3.

Answer
Two words made up of these letters, without additional letters, must be given.

TEST 24

Directions
You can give me words that begin with the same letters as break, bread, brain. (The experimenter holds up a card which has on it B R.) Now, give me three words that begin with D R. (The experimenter holds up a card with D R on it.) Write them here after one, two and three.

Form

24.

1.
2.
3.

Answer
Two words beginning with D R must be given.

TEST 25

Omitted because it is the same as 18.

TEST 26

Directions

I am going to read a sentence that has something foolish in it, some nonsense. Listen carefully and tell me what is foolish about it.

A little boy said, "I have three brothers, Paul, Ernest, and myself." Write the answer after one.

What is foolish about this? A little girl said, "If I look with one eye, I can see the street car when it is one block away. If I look with both eyes I ought to see it when it is two blocks away." Write the answer after two.

Form

26.

1.

2.

Answer

A sensible answer to one must be given.

TEST 27

Directions

This card has two drawings on it. I am going to show them ot you for twenty seconds, then I will take the card away and let you draw from memory what you have seen. Examine both drawings carefully and remember that you have only twenty seconds. (The experimenter exposes the drawings for twenty seconds.)

Form

27.

Answer

One of two correctly drawn. These are a little more complicated than the drawings used by Terman.

TEST 28

Directions

I am going to read something to you, and when I am through I want you to write as much as you can remember right here. A small boy / lives / on the street / in back / of my house /. He / always starts / for school / very early /. One day / he was late / for school / because / he stopped / to help / a blind man /. His teacher / excused him /. She said / he was / a good boy /. Write as much as you can here.

Form

28 a.

Answer

Six ideas must be correctly written down.

TEST 29

Directions

Write the answer to this question just below the question: "Why are there more policemen than firemen in a city?"

Write the answer to this question just below the question. "Why must we go to school when the school bell rings?"

Form

29 a.

Why are there more policemen than firemen in a city?

Why must we go to school when the school bell rings?

Answer

One of two must be correctly answered.
1. Usefulness, or variety of work.
2. Promptness, or not to miss any school work.

TEST 30

Directions

I am going to read you a word, and when I say it, I want you to write it here, and then write the two words of which you think first right after it. For example, if I say "cheese," you might write "eat plate." (The experimenter holds up a card with each of these words on it.)

Do you understand? Now listen—Table. (The experimenter holds up a card with "Table" on it.) Write the first two words you think of, down here.

Dark—(The experimenter holds up a card with "Dark" on it.) Write the first two words you think of, down here.

Music—(The experimenter holds up a card with "Music" on it.) Write the first two words you think of, down here.
Sickness—(The experimenter holds up a card with "Sickness" on it.) Write the first two words you think of, down here.
Man—(The experimenter holds up a card with "Man" on it.) Write the first two words you think of, down here.

Form

30 a.

Answer
At least three stimuli words must have been correctly responded to.

TIME ALLOWED

First Trial	Second Trial	Third Trial
	TEST 1	
2 minutes	1 minute	1 minute
	TEST 2	
30 seconds each	30 seconds each	30 seconds each
	TEST 3	
2 minutes	1 minute	1 minute
	TEST 4	
1 minute each	30 seconds each	30 seconds each
	TEST 5	
1 minute each	30 seconds each	30 seconds each
	TEST 6	
3 minutes each	3 minutes each	2 minutes each
	TEST 7	
1 minute	1 minute	1 minute
	TEST 8	
2 minutes each	1 minute each	1 minute each
	TEST 9	
5 seconds exposure	5 seconds exposure	5 seconds exposure
30 seconds to copy	30 seconds to copy	30 seconds to copy
	TEST 10	
4 minutes to make	4 minutes to make	4 minutes to make
	TEST 11	
2 minutes for first 1 minute for each of the others	1 minute each	1 minute each
	TEST 12	
1 minute each	30 seconds each	30 seconds each
	TEST 13	
1 minute	1 minute	1 minute

First Trial	Second Trial	Third Trial
	Test 14	
2 minutes	2 minutes	2 minutes
	Test 15	
1 minute each	30 seconds each	30 seconds each
	Test 16	
1 minute each	30 seconds each	30 seconds each
	Test 17	
1 minute each	1 minute each	1 minute each
	Test 18	
	About 15 minutes, each trial.	
	Test 19	
1 minute each	30 seconds each	30 seconds each
	Test 20	
1 minute	1 minute	1 minute
	Test 21	
1 minute each	30 seconds each	30 seconds each
	Test 22	
5 seconds exposure	5 seconds exposure	5 seconds exposure
30 seconds to copy	30 seconds to copy	30 seconds to copy
	Test 23	
3 minutes	3 minutes	3 minutes
	Test 24	
3 minutes	3 minutes	3 minutes
	Test 25	
	Omitted.	
	Test 26	
2 minutes each	2 minutes each	2 minutes each
	Test 27	
20 seconds exposure	20 seconds exposure	10 seconds exposure
1 minute to copy	1 minute to copy	1 minute to copy
	Test 28	
3 minutes to write	3 minutes to write	3 minutes to write
	Test 29	
2 minutes each	2 minutes each	2 minutes each
	Test 30	
1 minute each	1 minute each	1 minute each

APPENDIX III

MATERIAL FOR TRAINING THE "COACHED" GROUP

The only source used for this was the Stanford Revision of the Binet-Simon Tests, and its explanation in *The Measurement of Intelligence* by L. M. Terman (Houghton Mifflin Company, 1916). It was hoped that by using this one source only, and by coaching the children in the most obvious and straightforward manner, the methods used by an anxious parent in coaching a child would be duplicated rather well.

MATERIAL USED, AND DIRECTIONS

General Directions: Do not give all of the allotted time at once. Try to get the child to master the idea, and later come back if necessary for drill and re-inforcement.

SIX YEARS

1. Right and Left.

Correct answers for all six parts taught. Ten minutes was the maximum time to be devoted to this training.

The child was told to show the right hand, the left ear, the right hand, etc. If the confusion was marked, the child was informed that it was his right hand he used for writing. (All of these children had been taught to use only the right hand for writing.)

2. Mutilated Pictures.

Correct answers taught. Fifteen minutes was the maximum time. Further help was given by asking the child, "What must a face have?" "Now look and see what is gone here. Always look for all of the parts."

3. Count Thirteen Pennies.

The child was told the right number. Ten minutes was the maximum time.

If the child did not understand how to do it, the tester counted with the forefinger, and then said to the child, "Count with your finger, and tell me the last number you count."

4. Comprehension, Second Degree.

The answers were given to the child, who repeated them. Ten minutes was the maximum time.

The answers which were taught were:

a. Get an umbrella or a raincoat.

b. Get the firemen; break the fire-box.

c. Wait for the next car.

After the answers were fairly well established, the child was asked, "Why do you say that? Is that what you do?" in an effort to have the answers based on a little more than memoriter repetition.

5. Coins.

The names popularly used, and the values of the coins were taught. Five minutes was the maximum time.

6. Repeat Sixteen to Eighteen Syllables.

The child was given practice in saying each sentence correctly. Fifteen minutes was the maximum time.

The child was urged to do his best, and was constantly encouraged.

SEVEN YEARS

1. Fingers.

The child was practiced on saying five and five make ten. Ten minutes was the maximum time.

The fact that five and five make ten was made more real to the child by counting of pennies first, and then of fingers.

2. Pictures, Description or Better.

Practice in describing the picture was given. Fifteen minutes was the maximum time.

The child was helped by the examiner, who said "What is happening in this picture? Don't tell me the things you see, tell me what is happening, what the picture is about." Actual examples were given when necessary; as, "This little Dutch girl is crying, her mother is looking at her, and the cat is asleep."

3. Repeat Five Digits.

The child was practiced on each series at least ten times. The maximum time was fifteen minutes.

When the child was not able to do it then, he was shown a card with the numbers on it, and was practiced in saying the numbers after the card was removed. Then he was again given practice in saying them from dictation.

4. *Ties Bow Knot.*

Practice and help were given. Ten minutes was the maximum time. If the child could not tie a bow knot at all, the experimenter tied one for him several times very slowly and then guided his fingers through the process, pointing out the especially difficult places, and what to do with them. When the child finished, he was told to try it at home, and to be sure to learn it, for all big children could do it.

5. *Gives Differences.*

The child was taught two differences for each pair. Maximum time was ten minutes.

At least five repetitions of the differences were insisted upon. After these answers were fairly well established, the child was asked, "Why is that right?" and some attempt to teach him the reasons was made.

Any two of the differences for each pair were taught.

a. Color, size, wings, nuisance.

b. Hardness, cooking, edibility.

c. Breaking, transparency.

6. *Copies Diamond.*

The child was given practice in drawing this. The maximum time was fifteen minutes.

If the child's efforts were useless, he was given a diamond of the same dimensions as in the test booklet, and told to trace it, a line at a time, and to make nice sharp corners. After tracing five times, he again attempted it free-hand. If he still failed, he drew a diamond while the tester guided his hand and explained how to do it. Then once more he attempted to draw it free-hand.

EIGHT YEARS

1. *Ball and Field.*

The child was practiced on this. Five minutes was the maximum time.

The child was told, "You go around and around like this until you get to the middle, so you won't miss the ball anywhere. Now, you do it." At least four trials were given.

2. *Counts Twenty to Zero.*

Practice was given to those who were slow. Ten minutes was the maximum time given to this test.

If the child did not repeat the numbers fast enough, he was given enough practice to enable him to give them within the limit of forty seconds. If he did not understand the task he was shown a chart with the numbers from one to twenty in-clusive, and shown how to read them from twenty to one; then he was given practice in saying them with and without the chart.

3. *Comprehension, Third Degree.*

The answers were given to the child, who repeated them. Ten minutes was the maximum time.

The answers which were taught were:

a. Pay them for it, or get them a new one.

b. Run as fast as you can.

c. Don't do anything. Keep on playing.

After the answers were fairly established, the child was asked "Why must you do that?" in an attempt to get something more than a memoriter repetition of the answer.

4. *Gives Similarities, Two Things.*

The child was taught one similarity for each pair. The maxi-mum time was ten minutes.

At least five repetitions of the similarity were insisted upon. After these answers were fairly well established, the child was asked, "Why is that right?" and some attempt was made to have him understand the reason.

a. Both burn and are heavy.

b. Both grow, are fruit, are edible, and are colored alike.

c. Both are heavy, useful, and are metals.

d. Both go, carry things, and have motors.

5. *Definitions Superior to Use.*

The child was taught the specific answer. Ten minutes was the maximum time.

At least five repetitions were insisted upon. When the answers were fairly well established the child was told, "You must tell what sort of thing it is, and what it does."

a. A thing made of rubber that is blown up.

b. A wild animal that eats people.

c. A ball made of leather that you kick.

d. A man that marches and fights in the war.

6. *Vocabulary, Twenty Words.*

The simplest definition was taught for each of the forty words, twenty from each list. Thirty minutes was the maximum time.

These definitions were read to the children who repeated them. Where the definition was not understood, an example was given. After they had learned the definition for a word, it was dropped from the learning list, and those remaining were repeated again.

FIRST LIST

1. What you wear to bed at night.
2. To knock at the door.
3. To burn by getting a thing too hot.
4. A hole in the street with water in it.
5. What you use to put letters in to mail them.
6. Something you must do.
7. How your body is, sick or well.
8. Hair around the eye.
9. Metal to make wires and pennies.
10. To say bad words.
11. Meat from a pig. You eat it.
12. To go outside of some place.
13. In the south.
14. A meeting where you go to hear someone talk.
15. A dark place where you put prisoners.
16. Able to do a thing well.
17. To go around slowly.
18. Nice and polite.
19. To pay money, so that if you lose something you get paid for it.
20. Part of the body. It tells you how you feel.

SECOND LIST

1. A fruit that you eat.
2. A large fire that you have outside.
3. What horses use for a bed.
4. To make a loud noise.
5. To go quickly, to hurry.
6. To rest on top of the water.
7. To play on. It's like a banjo or a violin.
8. Soft and juicy.
9. Bad, not polite.
10. To fix the pipes and the sink.
11. Something that is easily seen.
12. What you put on a dog's mouth.
13. To shake; when the earth quakes.
14. A party where you meet people.
15. What you call a King.
16. Where you keep your money.
17. To use a thing badly, to hurt it.
18. To bite hard, and make a noise with your teeth.
19. To give up something because you made a mistake.
20. To feel like playing.

In all cases where the meaning was not clear to the child, actual instances were given until the child understood the definition at the time, even if he did not remember it later.

NINE YEARS

1. Actual present date was repeated. The maximum time was ten minutes.

The importance of knowing the date was stressed. A calendar was shown, and the child was told to look up the date every morning and to try to remember it. The date for the day of the training was repeated at least five times.

2. *Weights.*

Practice was given in handling them. Ten minutes was the maximum time.

If the child did not place them correctly at the end of three trials, the experimenter said, "Find the heaviest; lift them all, and find the heaviest. Good. Now lift all these, and find the heaviest. Put it beside the first one. Good. Now lift all these and find the heaviest. Put it here next to this one. Good. Now lift these two, and find the heaviest. Put it next in the row. Good. Now put the last one last in the row. Good. Do you understand? Do it again." These instructions were repeated if necessary.

3. *Makes Change.*

The child was told the right answers, and drilled in giving them. Five minutes was the maximum time.

4. *Repeats Four Digits Backwards.*

The child was given practice in saying the groups of four digits backwards. Ten minutes was the maximum time.

At least eight repetitions were required. If the child did not get them correctly, he was told to say the numbers the way the experimenter did, to himself, and then to say them backwards, slowly. If he still had difficulty, he was given a chart and shown how the numbers looked, told that they were read to him forwards, but that he must say them backwards. He was then given more practice in saying them backwards after they were dictated as usual.

5. *Three Words.*

Each series was put in a sentence which the child learned. Ten minutes was the maximum.

At least five repetitions were required. The sentences were as simple as possible. If the child had a half-formed sentence, that was improved and used.

a. The boy threw his ball in the river.
b. Men work to get money.
c. There are no rivers or lakes in the desert.

6. Rhymes.

Six rhymes were given for each word, which the child listened to, and was encouraged to repeat or add to. Ten minutes was the maximum time.

Both illustrations and practice were given. Poor rhymes and nonsense words were discarded, and the child told the reason.

TEN YEARS

1. Vocabulary.

Skipped, since practice in Year VIII-6 took care of this.

2. Absurdities.

The answers were taught and the child repeated them. Fifteen minutes was the maximum time.

At least five repetitions were required. An explanation was given for each absurdity, and the child was told to give the answer.

  a. He must go uphill going home.
  b. He would go more slowly.
  c. She couldn't cut herself in eighteen pieces.
  d. It was serious.
  e. He was dead.

3. Design.

The child was practiced in drawing these two designs. The maximum time was fifteen minutes.

The child traced the design five times, while the experimenter pointed out that the first design was equally tall, and that the second design had the center part on one side. Then the child drew with the card in front of him, and finally practiced drawing from memory.

4. Reading and Repetition.

The child was practiced in reading the passage within the required time limits. The maximum was twenty-five minutes.

The child was corrected for each error, and given enough practice to bring his reading time down to within thirty-five seconds. He was then called on to give a report of what he had read.

5. Comprehension, Fourth Degree.

The child learned the answers verbatim. The maximum time was fifteen minutes.

The answers which were taught were:
  a. "I don't know him very well."

b. Think it all over, plan it out.

c. Because we can see what he does, and he may not mean what he says.

After the answers were fairly well established the child was asked, "Why do you say that? That is right. Why is it a good answer?"

6. *Sixty Words.*

Practice in giving words fast. Ten minutes was the maximum time.

The child was given practice and encouragement. If he was not able to find thirty words in a minute he was helped by the experimenter, who said, "Give me all the words that belong to a house," and then "Give me all the words that belong to a farm," and then "Give me all the words that belong to a school," and later "Name all the fruits you can, all the animals."

Then the child was again given practice in saying as many words as possible.

TWELVE YEARS

This year was not used at A as part of the training, but it was thought advisable to add it as part of the work at Y.

1. *Vocabulary.*

Skipped, since practise had been given in Year VIII-6.

2. *Abstract Words.*

The right answers were repeated by the children. Ten minutes was the maximum time.

The answers were repeated at least six times. Examples were given for each word.

a. To be sorry for someone.

b. To get even with someone.

c. To give to the poor.

d. To want something that someone else has.

e. To give people what they deserve.

3. *Ball and Field.*

Skipped, since practice in Year VIII-1 took care of this.

4. *Dissected Sentences.*

Repetition of the right sentences. Fifteen minutes was the maximum time.

At least five repetitions were required. The words were pointed out in the proper order, and then the sentence was repeated.

5. Fables.

The right answer was repeated by the child. Fifteen minutes was the maximum time.

After the fable was read, the right answer was read to the child who repeated it two or three times. The fable was re-read and the child supplied the answer.

a. To help yourself before you call for help.
b. Not to plan too far ahead.
c. Not to be flattered.
d. Not to go in bad company.
e. To make up your mind and not let everybody change it.

6. Repeats Five Digits Backwards.

The child was given practice in saying the groups of five digits backwards. Ten minutes was the maximum time.

At least eight repetitions were required. If the child did not get them correctly, he was told to say the number the way the experimenter did, to himself, and then to say them backwards slowly. If he still had difficulty, he was given a chart and shown how the numbers looked, told that they were read to him forwards, but that he must say them backwards. He was then given more practice in saying them backwards after they were dictated as usual.

7. Pictures, Interpretation.

Practice in interpreting the pictures was given. Fifteen minutes was the maximum time.

The child was helped by the examiner, who said, "What do you think this picture means? What story does it tell?" Correct answers were read to the child who repeated them.

a. The mother hit the girl because she was naughty.
b. Two Indians are taking a man and a woman away. The woman is scared, so the man is holding her.
c. A man is reading the paper to four men. They are laughing at something funny about one of them. One man has come to sell eggs.
d. The man has to go away to war. His wife is afraid he'll be killed.

8. Gives Similarities, Three Things.

The child was taught one similarity for each set. The maximum time was ten minutes.

At least five repetitions of the similarity were insisted upon. After these answers were fairly well established, the child was asked, "Is that right?" The experimenter tried to show him the reason for the answer.

a. All are animals.
b. All teach you something.
c. All are used for clothing.
d. All are hard material.
e. All grow from the ground.